AFRICA AND AFRICANS IN THE NEW TESTAMENT

David Tuesday Adamo

University Press of America,® Inc.
Lanham · Boulder · New York · Toronto · Oxford

Copyright © 2006 by
University Press of America,® Inc.
4501 Forbes Boulevard
Suite 200
Lanham, Maryland 20706
UPA Acquisitions Department (301) 459-3366

PO Box 317
Oxford
OX2 9RU, UK

All rights reserved
Printed in the United States of America
British Library Cataloging in Publication Information Available

Library of Congress Control Number: 2005929541

ISBN: 978-0-7618-3302-4

⊖™ The paper used in this publication meets the minimum
requirements of American National Standard for Information
Sciences—Permanence of Paper for Printed Library Materials,
ANSI Z39.48—1984

DEDICATION

This book is dedicated to my family: my beloved wife, Grace Ebunlola Adamo, my sons, Oluwayomi Bamidele, and David Tuesday Jr., and my daughters, Pauline Bolutife and Oluwaremilekun, who suffered my absence while I was in the United States writing this book.

Table of Contents

Preface   v

Acknowledgments   vii

PART ONE: GENERAL INTRODUCTION   1

Chapter I: Introduction   3

Chapter II: Africa and Africans and the Formation of the New Testament   9

Chapter III: Terms Used to Refer to Africa and Africans in the New Testament   21

Chapter IV: How Egypt became a Melting Pot   37

PART TWO: AFRICA AND AFRICANS IN THE GOSPELS   49

Chapter V: Africa and Africans in the Gospel of Matthew   51

Chapter VI: Africa and Africans in the Gospel of According to Mark   69

PART THREE: AFRICA AND AFRICANS IN THE ACTS OF THE APOSTLES AND THE EPISTLES   77

Chapter VII: Africa and Africans in Jerusalem   79

Chapter VIII: Africa and Africans in Antioch	87
Chapter IX: Africa and Africans in Philippi, Ephesus, and Corinth	95
Chapter X: Africa and Africans in the Epistle to the Rome	107
Chapter XI: Conclusion	113
Bibliography	117
Index	123

PREFACE

In 1968 when I started my theological education at Igbaja Bible College (now ECWA Bible College), Igbaja, Nigeria, I never knew that I would reach this stage in life. Throughout the eight years I spent at ECWA Bible College and Seminary, I was taught by dedicated evangelical educators, none of them ever gave me a hint that there was a presence of Africa and Africans in the pages of the Old and New Testament Bible. Neither did my education at Perkins School of Theology, Southern Methodist University, and Baylor University give me the knowledge of the idea of African presence in the Bible.

But thank God, I had the opportunity to participate in an archaeological excavation at Tel 'Ira, in Israel in 1981 when I was pursuing my PhD in Religion at Baylor University. It was then that I knew that even in Modern Hebrew language, the word *Cush,* so frequent in the Hebrew Bible, means "black" and is one of the terms that refer to African people in the Bible. It was then that I decided to investigate the word in the Hebrew Bible. After the publication of my revised dissertation and my subsequent teaching of a course (Africa and Africans in the Biblical Period) at Perkins School of Theology in Dallas, my students encouraged me to write a book on the subject. They were overwhelmed with so much information about the biblical presence of Africa and Africans. One of them asked me, "Why can't they teach us this information? "You have written a book on the Old Testament, what about the New Testament?" I felt an obligation to answer the above questions and accepted them as a challenge.

What I have done in this book therefore, is to first examine critically, the role of Africa and Africans in the formation of the New Testament books. In order to be able to know the exact references to Ancient Africa and Africans I also try to determine the various terms used to refer to Ancient Africa and Africans in the New Testament.

The book is divided into three parts. The first is the general introduction which contains the introduction, the formation of the New Testament and the various terms for Africa and Africans. The second is the critical examination of the Gospels which contains the critical discussion of each reference to Ancient Africa and Africans in the Gospels. Part third deals with Africa and Africans in the Acts of the Apostles and the Epistles.

My hope is that this book will reveal new facts about the presence and the contribution of ancient Africa and Africans in the New Testament Bible. I also hope that it will stimulate Africentric and Eurocentric biblical scholars to do further useful research on this subject.

    Professor David Tuesday Adamo PhD
    Delta State University
    Abraka, Delta State
    Nigeria

ACKNOWLEDGMENTS

I must first all thank my wife, Grace Ebunlola Adamo of the Department of English and Literary Studies, Delta State University, Abraka, Nigeria, who edited this manuscript. She deserves the greatest praise and thanks.

My gratitude also goes to Perkins School of Theology, who allowed me to teach a course titled, "Africa and Africans in the Biblical Period." My students in that class also deserve my appreciation for their encouragement. I am particularly grateful to Tara Kiene, my best student, who read the entire manuscript and did some corrections. I am also grateful to Pauline Logan who encouraged me to complete the manuscript. She also read the manuscript and did some corrections.

I am also grateful to my colleagues and good friends, Rev. Fr. Professor Justin Ukpong, Department of Religious Studies, University of Uyo, Uyo, Nigeria, Joseph Enuwosa, Delta State University, Abraka, Nigeria, and Dr. Knut Holter, School of Mission and Theology, Stavanger, Norway, who went through the manuscript. Dr. (Mrs) 'Ronke Olajubu, Dr. Olu Alana of the Department of Religions, University of Ilorin, Nigeria deserve my gratitude for going through the manuscript. My son, David Tuesday Adamo Jnr who read this manuscript also deserves my appreciation. Professor Cain Hope Felder, The 'Divinity School, Howard University, Washington D.C, deserves my appreciation for editing part of this manuscript. My doctoral student, Pastor Senne-Aya who also read this manuscript deserves my appreciation. I am grateful to African Baptist Church of Irving who allowed me to spend my sabbatical leave as the pastor of the church

This acknowledgement cannot be complete without mentioning those who have contributed to my success in my educational struggle. The first people are Catholic mission and the Headmaster of RCM Primary school Itedo-Isanlu, Kogi State, Mr.R.O Awuto (1960), who after seeing my commitment and determination to be educated, gave me admission despite my failure to pass entrance examination. I appreciate ECWA Bible College and Seminary, Igbaja and especially their missionaries who taught me discipline and biblical interpretation. I am grateful to Indiana Christian University, Indianapolis and Baylor University, Waco, Texas USA. All the United Methodist Churches (First United Methodist Church, Waco, St Philip United Methodist Church, First United Methodist Church, Quanah and others in Texas who assisted me financially deserve my praise.

Professor FMA Ukoli, the first Vice Chancellor of Delta State University, who insisted that I must be appointed as a Professor of Religious Studies in 1983 is greatly appreciated. His objectivity and appreciation of excellent and international scholarship is commendable.

My university, Delta Sate University, also deserves appreciation because of my sabbatical leave that enabled me complete this book.

Without the assistance of these people mentioned above, this book would have been impossible.

    Thank God for everything.
    David Tuesday Adamo PhD

PART ONE:

GENERAL INTRODUCTION

CHAPTER I

INTRODUCTION

The examination of the presence of Africa and Africans in the Bible is fairly recent. Increasing number of Africans and African Americans has begun to note that many Eurocentric biblical scholars have the tendency to "deAfricanize" the Bible over the years. That process seems to have begun with "deAfricanization" of ancient Egypt. For the Euro-American guild, Egypt has been transformed into a virtually European country and belongs to ancient Near East and not Africa. The denial of the presence of Africa and Africans has suddenly rather effective and demoralizing because people have tended to trust the claims of biblical scholarship in the hand of these Eurocentric scholars. The fact is that most of the translations of the Bible,[1] reputable Bible commentaries, textbooks on introduction to the Bible, Bible Atlases, Bible dictionaries and encyclopedia, theology of the Old and New Testaments, history of the Old and New Testaments, archaeology of the Bible land, and other important subjects are written by western scholars.

I believe that the situation above would have improved if Africans in the Diaspora had been taught how to read very early. Unfortunately when they were taught and given the opportunity to be educated, they were given inferior education. Let me illustrate this as far as Africans in their homeland are concerned. In the late sixties and seventies, some Africans were allowed to go to one of the universities in Europe. They were given the so-called special education and given special degrees and diplomas in fewer years. On the degrees/certificates/diplomas were written, "for work in Africa only." In other words, these degrees, diplomas and certificates were not valid for use in European countries.[2] This means that even when Africans were given some education, they were given inferior education.

Certainly, there would have been a difference in the domination of biblical scholarship if African Americans had been given the opportunity to be converted and to learn to read and write very early. I can recall reading about the situation in the United States recounted by Johnstone:

> Early in Colonial American history the question arose concerning what to do about the religion of black slaves. One mandate said: Convert them to Christianity. But the other said: You shouldn't hold a fellow Christian as a slave. Therefore, what to do? Some slave-owners quite expectedly opposed the conversion of slaves. Unconverted they presented no problem, since the slave-owners would not be holding a fellow Christian as a slave. But theologians and clergymen said it is the Christian's obligation to teach the slaves Christianity and convert them. Some Southerners resolved the issue by defining blacks as less than human. We don't convert dogs, kudus or zebra; therefore, we don't need to convert blacks: as a lower animal form, they lack a soul to be saved.[3]

The situation in the United States was inhuman. I can again recall one of my professor's comments in one of the doctoral classes about the African Americans. He said with all seriousness, that the slave owners knew very well that the African Americans were very brilliant people. The white men knew that if they had been taught how to read and write or allowed in to the higher institutions very early, and had been allowed to participate in professional boxing, football, and other important games, they would have dominated America by now. That is why they denied them this opportunity. What I am saying is that, if the African Americans had been allowed in the major seminaries and divinity schools very early, the domination of the biblical scholarship by the Eurocentric scholars would have been impossible.

Although the Hebrew Bible is primarily the record of and a witness to the revelation of the act of God within a particular nation (Israel), it also recognizes God's involvement with other nations such as Africans (Ethiopians), Assyrians, Babylonians, Edomites, Syrians and others. This is because ancient Israel interacted with these nations. The New Testament, like the Old Testament, is also a record of God's revelation concerning the great redemption He has accomplished through a particular people (Jews). The New Testament however, is not limited to the Jews, but extended to other nations. God used, not only the Jews, but also other nations for the spread of the Gospel of redemption.

While the role played by many of these nations has been examined, that of Africa and Africans has not been adequately researched. Although there are researches on Egypt and the Old and New Testaments by western scholars, it was done with the premeditated opinion that Egypt is not part of Africa and presumably the idea that nothing good can come from Africa, south of the Sahara.

The purpose of this book is to investigate the presence and the role of Africa and Africans in the New Testament time. In order to do this successfully it is imperative to extend the boundaries of African history to include African Diaspora during the New Testament time. This is necessary because this method of expanding the boundaries of Africa and Africans to include African Diaspora has been so neglected by historians and biblical scholars. No nation's achievement has been attributed to other nations like that of Africa. I feel that this is an important issue which biblical scholars must tackle so that the problem of attributing Africa and African's contribution to other nations can be reduced. I therefore regard all people of African descent as "Africans," regardless whether they are Jews and live in Africa or not. It should be noted that I call all Africans at home and outside the continents of Africa, Africans, regardless of methods of how they got there (either by slavery or boat or voluntary or air). This will assist us to discover, recognize, and bring to the knowledge of the world the contribution of Africa and Africans in the New Testament period as recorded in the pages of the New Testament Bible.

This book is also an attempt to challenge biblical and other kinds of academic racism, neo-colonization, and the policy of de-Africanization of the Bible as practiced by the majority of Eurocentric scholars. In addition, this book attempts to answer the questions: is it correct to say that western missionaries and explorers brought Christianity to Africa? Is Christianity a White man's religion as some people claim? Why did the biblical writers take time always to give specific identification to the people of African descent as people from Africa whenever they are mentioned in the pages of the New Testament? Why is the church growing geometrically, that is, at the rate of 16,400 Christians per day in Africa?[4] Why did Dr. Kwame Bediako, refers to Africa as the "laboratory of the world" as far as Christianity is concerned?[5]

In order to achieve this purpose, I have examined the various references and terms used to refer to Africa and Africans in the New Testament. The word "Egypt" is the leading term used in the New Testament to refer to Africa and Africans. The fact is that the word "Egypt" occurs seven hundred and forty (740) times in the Old Testament. In the New Testament Bible it occurs more than 40 times. Unlike the some western scholars who see Egypt as part of Europe, it is more appropriate to consider Egypt as part and parcel of Africa.

The word Ethiopia is also examined tracing the meaning of the use of the word from the Old Testament to the New Testament times. The word that was translated Ethiopia in the Old Testament scripture is "*Cush.*" This word with its cognates occurs 77 times in the Old Testament, but was translated in the King James Version to Ethiopia fifty-eight times.[6] It also occurs in the New Testament Bible.

The word Libya or Phut or Punt that occurs about 7 times in the Old Testament, also occurs many times in the New Testament. Cyrene and Cyrenians were also mentioned in the pages of the New Testament. They refer to the same country of Libya and her people.

The fact that must be emphasized is that references to Africa and Africans in the pages of the Old and New Testaments are about 867 times. No other nations, except Israel, were mentioned so frequently like Africa (not even the

Assyria and Assyrians or Babylon and Babylonians). This is as a result of God's love for Africa and their participation in the eternal redemption wrought by God as recorded in the pages of the Scripture. That is the reason it is absolutely necessary to examine Africa and Africans in the pages of the Bible.

In the following pages, I argued that Africa has been a place of refuge, not only to the savior, but also throughout the biblical history as documented by the Bible and archaeology. I also discussed the fact that Africa and Africans have been worshippers of Yahweh, God of Israel, and have been in possession of the written Scripture of the Old Testament before the New Testament was ever written. They were present and were represented at the cross of Calvary and even carried the cross. Very strongly, Africa and Africans with their unusual enthusiasm and zeal have been at the forefront in the preaching of the Gospels of Jesus Christ and the expansion of early Christianity in the New Testament. They were teachers and prophets in the period of the Old and New Testament. Perhaps, the authors of Matthew, Mark, Luke, John and Acts could be Africans as will be discussed later in this book. During the biblical times, many Africans became Jews and took up even their citizenry as a mark of their zeal and religiosity. The Jewry of the authors of the New Testament should not stop them from the possibility of being Africans. Evidences of the many black orthodox Jews are being discovered daily in Africa, such as the Falashas in present country of Ethiopia and also the Lembas in South Africa. These evidences are fully discussed in the book.

This book is an attempt to present a different perspective on the history during the New Testament period because of the great distortion that has gone into African history in the biblical period. At this time Africa and African Diaspora cannot wait for people who deliberately distorted African past due to their prejudice and racism to put it in proper perspective for them. As said earlier in my former book, *Africa and Africans in the Old Testament*, it is also necessary for my readers to relax whatever might be their past and present conception about Africa and Africans and listen to other radical new opinions, whether they are acceptable to them or not, different from the mainline Eurocentric interpretation of the scripture. Again, I will congratulate myself (to use the words of Dr. Cain Felder) if this book only helps to trouble someone's mind as one reads and interpret the Bible Africentrically.[7]

My hope is that this book will stimulate other African biblical scholars to write more on this subject.

Endnotes

[1] Thank God for few African American scholars who have embarked on some translation of the Bible.
For example, *Holy Bible, African American Edition* published by the American Bible Society, New York is an important project. *Original African Heritage Bible*, edited by Cain Hope Felder is another good example of all effort to translate the Bible Afrocentically.

[2] My readers should please permit me to withhold the names of some of the universities in England.

[3] R.L Johnstone, *Religion and Society in Interaction* (Englewood Cliffs: Prentice-Hall, Inc. 1975), 218

[4] Ronald A. Nathan, "Pan-Africanism: What of the Twenty-First Century? A British Perspective," *Black Theology in Britain*, Issue 4, 2000, 19.

[5] Kwame Bediako, *Christianity in Africa*, 252

[6] F.D Gealy, "Ethiopia," *Interpreters' Bible*, vol. 2 (George A Buttrick, gen. ed. (Nashville: Abingdon Press, 1962),176-177.

[7] Cain Hope Felder, *Troubling Biblical Waters: Race, Class. and Family* (Maryknoll, New York: Orbis Books, 1989*)*.

CHAPTER II

AFRICA AND AFRICANS AND THE FORMATION OF THE NEW TESTAMENT

In the previous chapter I discussed various terms used to refer to Africa and Africans in the New Testament. I discussed elaborately the case of Egypt and Alexandria. In this chapter it is important to refresh your memories about my understanding of Egypt and Alexandria. The entire countries of North Africa are African countries inhabited by African people before the colonization by various foreign people such as the Hyksos, Assyrians, Persians, Greeks, Romans and Great Britain. The Pharaohs mentioned in the books of the Old Testament were black Africans, except some of the Asiatic pharaohs who colonized the countries during the biblical period. Although black people still remain there, most of them were pushed to the southern countries. This untold, long-time colonization and domination actually affected the pigmentation of their skin. Colonization is still going on in academic circles for it has been successful in making the world at large believe that North Africa, particularly Egypt, is not part of Africa, but Europe. This is what is called neo-colonization today. I will like to emphasize again that I consider North Africa, particularly Egypt, as part of African continent. Those who were born, lived, and worked in that part of the continent were Africans. I have to refresh my readers' memories concerning this since most of the people who contributed to the formation of the New Testament that I would discuss in this chapter were born, lived and worked in that part of Africa.

Mark and Barnabas in Africa.

We may be able to put together the life of St. Mark, the cousin and close associate of Barnabas (Acts 12:39). The son of Peter and co-worker of Paul were simply known as Mark. John Mark's association with Peter goes back to the house of Mary (Acts. 12:1ff) in Jerusalem. Papias mentioned that Mark, as a follower of and interpreter of Peter 'wrote down accurately that entire he remembered of the things said and done by the Lord.' Mark was converted and probably baptized by Peter because the Monarchian Prologue to the Gospel of Mark describes Mark as a Levite who was converted by Peter.

The Gospel of Mark that first recorded the episode of Simon is associated with African Christians. Egyptian Coptic Christians claimed that Mark the author of this Gospel is the founder of their church and is the first patriarch. They maintain that the Gospel of Mark was brought to Egypt in Greek language and when the Egyptian Christians could not read Greek, it was translated to Egyptian language. Coptic traditions also maintain that Mark established a Christian mission in Egypt, Cyrenaica, and in other Libyan cities.[1]

The movement of Barnabas, though more obscure than that of Mark, can be seen according to the Bible. Barnabas returned to Cyprus with Mark (Acts. 15:39). In 1 Cor. 9:6, Paul mentioned Barnabas as serving as a missionary. Paul also mentioned him in Galatians 2: 9 as alive. Barnabas may have come in contact with Apollos at Alexandria by 50-53CE giving him allot of encouragement to become a missionary in the Aegean area. The conciliatory nature of Barnabas was written in Galatians 2:13, Acts. 4:36, and 11:22-24. There was a reference to Barnabas during the division into parties, namely, Apollos, Paul, Cephas and Christ in I Cor. 9:6.

The attribution of an Epistle to Barnabas by tradition, and the so many references to him show that he was in Africa-Egypt. Among these references in the Epistle to Barnabas are 1:1,3,4, 2:8; 4:6,9; 6:5; 9:9 and 21:7. Clement of Alexandria quoted it seven times as written by Barnabas. He has a very keen interest in Barnabas himself. He referred to him as 'the Apostle' Barnabas,' (Strom. ii.6, 31, 7: 35) and as a member of the Seventy (Strom.ii: 20). The Clementine *Homilies* (i: 7.14, 9 and ii: 4) reported Barnabas visit to Alexandria and his preaching there when he was on his way from Antioch to Rome. Alexander, the Monk, also mentioned the tradition that Barnabas preached in Alexandria in the sixth century.[2]

Acts.15: 39 recorded that Barnabas took Mark with him on a journey to Cyprus following an argument with Paul concerning Mark's fitness. Barnabas believed that Mark was ready for more responsibility even though Paul was not convinced. This action must have restored Mark's confidence and sealed his association with Barnabas. When they parted, Paul and Silas went northwest while Mark and Barnabas went southwest (Acts. 15:39-41). Cyprus was on the way from Antioch to Egypt and was on a direct line. This would have been a suitable place for Barnabas and Paul to visit because of the presence of the Hellenists associated with Alexandria through Stephen in Cyprus.

Another suitable place for Mark to visit is Cyrene since Lucius of Cyrene was one of the prophets in Antioch who laid hands on Barnabas and Paul and commissioned them for a missionary journey to Cyprus and Asia Minor (Act. 13:1-3). According to Acts 11:18-30, Cyrenian refugees were among the founders of the church in Antioch. If Barnabas was sent to Cyprus from Antioch will he also not go to Cyrene because there were many Cyrenians and Cypriotes Hellenists in Antioch? Mark 15:21 mentioning Simon of Cyrene, the father of Alexander and Rufus shows that Mark knew some Cyrenians personally because Cyrenians Jews were very familiar with Jerusalem.

Mark was associated with Alexandria. Clement of Alexandria in his Letter to Theodore, and Jerome in his Latin version of the Chronicle of Eusebius (Migne, PG. 539) reported that Mark, the Evangelist, the interpreter of Peter, proclaimed Christ in Egypt and in Alexandria.[3] When Clement of Alexandria wrote to Theodore he reported that when Peter was murdered, Mark came to Alexandria and left for the Church of Alexandria the more spiritual Gospel which he and Peter had composed for advanced Christians.[4] John Chrysostom, citing Eusebius, after citing I Peter 5:13 say, "And they say (phasim) this Mark was the first to be sent to preach in Egypt the Gospel which he had written, and he first established churches in Alexandria."[5] He continued, "In the eighth year of the reign of Nero (62-63), Annianus was the first to succeed Mark the Evangelist in the custody of the community in Alexandria."[6]

From the above, one may safely conclude that the Gospel of Mark was probably written in Africa, namely, Alexandria. It certainly bears an Alexandrian's mark.

Matthew, Luke, the Fourth Gospel, and Africa.

As I have discussed, the possibility of Africa being the origin of the book of Mark, so also I want to discuss the possibility of Matthew's, Luke's and the Gospel of John's origin in Africa. I have also discussed the origin of Alexandrian Christianity. From the evidence already discussed previously, I said that by the second century, there existed a large flourishing church in Alexandria distinguished by the vigor of its intellectual life. The reference to Apollos from Alexandria and his defective knowledge of the new faith by Pauline standards, demonstrate that Christianity was brought to Alexandria by persons who had learned their faith in Jerusalem and who continued to be loyal to the church in Jerusalem as the mother church.[7] Dr. Brandon has suggested correctly that the Gospel of Matthew was composed in Africa-Alexandria after 70CE when she had become the sole inheritor of Jerusalem tradition. Matthew's interest in the story of the flight to Egypt, the strong Judaistic interest of the Gospel, and the elevation of Peter who was closely associated with Alexandria support this theory.

The Fourth Gospel was probably written in Africa-Alexandria. As early as 135 CE the Fourth Gospel was well known in Africa.[8] In fact, more texts of the Fourth Gospel have been found in Egypt than even Mark or Luke. There were seven of John's and nine of Matthew's. The strong Philonic flavor found in the prologue of the Fourth Gospel support that it was written or composed in Africa. It shows that the author probably belonged to the Alexandrian church and held Alexandrian theology. The Fragment of an Unknown Gospel discovered in Egypt, which belonged to the first half of the second century, contains several passages, which can be parallel in the Fourth Gospel.[9] There are also some paralleled passages in Matthew, Mark, and Luke but not as many in each of these Gospels, like that of the Fourth Gospel. Its discovery in Egypt shows that it was written in Alexandria and for Alexandrian and Egyptian communities. Another evidence that supports that the Fourth Gospel was written in Alexandria was the accounts in the Fourth Gospel and that of Matthew. The first account is in John 1:8.

This passage says, "He was not that Light, but was sent to bear witness of that Light." The Fourth Gospel never mentions that John baptized Jesus, nor make any mention of any real meeting and conversation between Jesus and John. In these passages: "Again the next day after John stood and two of his disciples, and looking upon Jesus, as he walked, he saith, 'behold the Lamb of God." And the two disciples heard him speak, and they followed Jesus"(1:29). Thus, the Fourth Gospel reduces the role of John the Baptist to that of a testimonial when he sighted someone he had not seen before but was revealed to him by the Spirit.

Matthew's account of Jesus' baptism shows that it belongs to the same milieu where it was necessary to explicitly assert the claims of Jesus over that of John. Matthew alone of the Synoptic Gospel gives an account of the

conversation between Jesus and John and John testifies to the Messiahship of Jesus. But John forbade him, saying, I have need to be baptized of thee, and comest thou to me? And Jesus answering said unto him, Suffer it to be so now for thus it becometh us to fulfil all righteousness. Then he suffered him (Matthew 3:14-15). The passages in the Fourth Gospel and Matthew, when compared with the records of Mark and Luke, show that the Fourth Gospel and Matthew belong to the place where there was a dispute about Jesus' relationship with John, that is, Alexandria.[10]

It has been generally accepted that Luke is the author of the books of Luke and Acts of the Apostles. What is fascinating to me is the place and attention given to Africa and Africans by Luke in the Acts of the Apostles. The book of the Acts of Apostles recorded activities in Africa and by Africans more than any other book of the New Testament. The presence of Africans on the day of Pentecost (Acts 2:13, 37-41), the Egyptians and Alexandrians were mentioned as participating in that meeting, Luke recorded Stephen narrating the events that took place in Africa at the time of Moses. He also mentioned the fact that those who opposed and instigated people against Stephen were his own people, Africans. Great attention was accorded to the African minister of finance the so-called "Ethiopian Eunuch." I am sure that he was not the only person who went to Jerusalem for pilgrimage. It is very likely that people from other nations participated. Of all the foreigners who went for worship in Jerusalem, this rich African man was the only one Luke seemed to have interest in. Why? Luke may be writing from Africa or he may be an African himself. It is amazing that Luke deliberately and persistently mentioned and identified Africans as prophets and teachers (Acts 13:1). He identified Simeon called, Niger, and Lucius from Cyrene and that they laid hand on Apostle Paul before he went on his missionary journey. Luke was very enthusiastic in identifying Apollos, the great teacher and missionary to Ephesus and Corinth. He was described as eloquent and fervent in spirit (Acts 18:24-28). Luke did not leave out African woman. He identified Lydia who was in Philippi and her generosity to Paul and his companion (Acts 16:14-15, 40). Why such great interest of Luke in African people if he was not writing from Africa or if he is not himself a native African? Despite the many disputes and controversies, and doubt by the Eurocentric biblical scholars, I hold very firmly that Luke could have been an African probably from Alexandria or from another African nation.

From the above, it is very likely that the Gospels of Matthew, Mark, and John were written in Africa. Perhaps, the authors of these books were Africans.

Africa and Africans' Contribution to the Formation of the Books of the New Testament

The process of the formation of the books of the New Testament is what scholars refer to as canonicity. Canonicity means the process by which the books of the Bible were gathered together as authoritative books and were accepted by the early Christian community. The important fact is that Africa and Africans are not left out in this development. After much prayer, fasting, and debate, they were collected, approved, and accepted. It means that the books of the New Testament were not merely gathered together and forced on the early Christian Church community. Some criteria were set and were guided by those criteria. Among this criterion is the apostolic origin of the books, general acceptability by the Christian community that received the letters, and the conformity to the rule of faith.

During the development of the formation of the New Testament Africa and Africans participated in the process. Among these eminent Africans are Pantaenus, Clement of Alexandria, Origen, Tertullian, Cyprian of Carthage and others. Although these eminent scholars are Africans, the majority of Western scholars attributed their contributions to the West. One of the ways in which this was done was to consider North Africa as part of Europe. As stated in the previous chapter, the entire North Africa belongs to Africa and was inhabited by Africans before the colonization of the people from Asia and Europe (read my discussion on Egypt and Libya in the previous chapter).

Events that Influenced the Formation of the New Testament.

One of the important events that influenced the formation of the New Testament is the rise of Gnosticism. This is a syncretistic religion and philosophy that came up alongside early Christianity. It teaches that one can gain salvation through special knowledge *gnosis*. This movement developed extensive literature for the purpose of instructing its believers. It made extensive use of the New Testament to justify its teaching. This extensive Gnostic literature challenged the early Christians to gather together the various books of the New Testament that were considered authentic and authoritative because their teaching was considered anti-Christian.

Basilides

One of the earliest Gnostic scholars is an African scholar called Basilides. He lived and taught in the famous Africa University in the city of Alexandria. He taught that Jesus did not actually die on the cross. He lent His form to the African man called Simon of Cyrene who immediately looked like Jesus in his appearance. Jesus then took up Simon's body and stood near the cross and laughed at the people who were crucifying Simon and taught that they were crucifying Jesus. His writing was influential.

Carpocrates and Valentinus

Carpocrates was an African Platonist and Gnostic who lived in the city of Alexandria in Africa. Velentinus was also an African who lived in Egypt. He later moved to Rome and established a Gnostic school that influenced many Christians. His many writings also rivaled Christian literature. The Library of writing called Nag Hamadi documents is the great document of the Gnostic teaching found in Africa.

Collection of Orphic fragments were also published with an elaborate discussion on the uniqueness of the literature. All these collection of literature influenced and challenged the Christian Church to collect and develop which books of the New Testament were genuine and authoritative.

The Development of the Formation of the New Testament

During the development of the New Testament canon, Africa and Africans made valuable contributions to this development. Many African scholars have made very valuable contributions to the development of the formation of the New Testament books. Scholars such as Pantaenus, Clement of Alexandria, Origen, Tertullian, and Cyprian of Carthage are important African figures of that time.

Pantaenus

Pantaenus was the first head of the African catechetical school in Alexandria. Although his nativity was not clearly known, he was likely from one of the cities of North Africa where he lived and worked.[11] Pantaenus vigorously defended the Pauline authorship of the book of Hebrews as an authentic book.

Clement of Alexandria

Clement of Alexandria who was a pulpit of Pantaenus was another African scholar whose nativity Western Scholars attributed to Greece instead of Africa. There was no clear evidence to support Athens as his place of nativity. Although he traveled extensively to East and West, he spent most of his fruitful life in the city of Alexandria and as the head of the African University in Alexandria. Clement accepted the Pauline authorship of the book of Hebrews and accepted the importance of religious knowledge to the chief element in Christian perfection. He quoted extensively from the book of the Old and New Testaments, classical, and apocryphal writings for about 8,000 times. He used the word canon about twenty times.[12] Although he did not apply it to the collection of books, he spelt out the books that were acceptable and authoritative and the ones that were not. He cited all the books of the New Testament, except James, Philemon, 2 Peter, and 2 and 3 John.

Origen

Origen was an African scholar born in Egypt about 185 CE. At the age of 18 he was appointed to succeed Clement of Alexandria as the head of the University of Alexandria. Among the ante-Nicene scholars, he was the greatest as a theologian and biblical scholar. He was a biblical scholar *par excellence*. He later moved to Caesarea and established a new biblical and theological school as a result of persecution in Alexandria. Apart from the textual work on the Old Testament called, *Hexapla*, he commented on almost all the books of the Bible. He divided the books of the New Testament into two: the Gospel or the Gospels and the Apostles or Apostles. He merged them together as the NT divine "Scriptures." According to him, they were written by evangelists and Apostles through the Holy Spirit and were acceptable and authoritative.

Tracing the development of the formation of the New Testament in the West, we also found many African scholars such as Scillitan Martyrs, Tertullian,

Cyprian of Carthage who made substantial contribution to the development of the canon.

Didymus the Blind

He is another celebrated African teacher and head of the Alexandria University for more than half a century. Though he was a layman who became blind at the age of four, he became a celebrated African teacher and head of the Alexandrian University for more than half a century. He made use of his powerful memory by memorizing most portions of the Bible. He dictated to his secretaries a lot of portions of the Bible during his exegetical works. A lot of his works was accidentally discovered in 1941 at Toura, south of Cairo in Egypt. These works contained a group of papyrus codices comprising nearly about two thousand pages.

He cited from all the books of the New Testament except Philemon and 2 and 3 John. This seems to mean that he did not accept the books of the Epistle of John and Philemon as canonical. He cited other books such as I Clement, Epistle of Barnabas, Didache and Shepherd of Hermas.

Acts of Scillitan Martyrs

In the history of the Latin Church, the Acts of the Scillitan Martyrs remain the oldest document. It is a document written with "moving sobriety."It concerns the story of the bravery and courage of seven men and five women from the village of Scillitan, Numidia in the present Tunisia, North Africa, who stood trial in Carthage on July 17, 180 CE for their faith. They professed their faith and refused to worship the emperor before they were executed. During their trial, they held in their bag some books. When they were asked what was in their bag, they boldly answered that they were books and "Epistles of Paul, a good man." Their devotion to the books of the Bible, including the Epistles of Paul became widely known and were widely publicized to be important books and worth devotion and belief.

Tertullian

Quintus Septimus Florence Tertullianus was one of the outstanding early African theologians. He was born in Carthage, in North Africa. Tertullian also had a great influence on the development of the formation of the New Testament. Tertullian was among great Montanist scholars. The greatest contribution of Tertullian to the development of the canon was the attention paid to the scope of the New Testament, which he accepted, and the time devoted to counteract the Marcionite canonicity. [13] Tertullian was the most prolific Latin Fathers of his period. He cited all the books of the New Testament books as authoritative except 2 Peter, James, 2 and 3 John. He regarded the Old

Testament scriptures as divinely given. He constantly denounced Marcion who refused to accept the Acts of Apostles. He defended every book of the Epistles one by one against Marcion.[14]

Montanist produced some literatures classified as "sacred" scriptures. Other African scholars in the African library of Alexandria collected certain writings of early authors and published them as scriptures or standard editions. The so-called Alexandrian Canon was developed in the city of Alexandria.

Cyprian of Carthage

Caecilius Cyprianus of Carthage became bishop of Carthage two years after his conversion by the acclamation of his people. He was "a rich and master of eloquence in Carthage" before he was converted to Christianity.[15] He was eventually placed as the head of the whole North African clergy. He administered very brilliantly, the episcopal office in Carthage. He seems to have memorized the entire scriptures. Of the 7,966 verses in the New Testament, he quoted 886 verses (about one-ninth of the entire New Testament). His New Testament, according to his reconstruction, contained the four Gospels, the Pauline Epistles, I Peter, I John and the Apocalypse.[16] He cited 934 biblical quotations from both the Old Testament and the New Testament and used them about 1,499 times in various contexts.[17]

Athanasius

Athanasius was born between 296-298 CE in Egypt. He was educated at the African University in Alexandria. He was one of the "key ecclesiastical and theological leaders of the church in the 4th century, He read and commented on every book of the Bible. He later became the bishop of Alexandria. His major contribution has to do with his commentary on every book of the Bible and his polemical work against the Arians who taught that the Son was different in essence from the Father. According to him, the Son was a created being.[18] His commentary on the books of the Bible assisted the church in authenticating which books of the New Testament were to be regarded as canonical.

Augustine of Hippo

He was born in North Africa to a Christian Mother called Monica who fervently prayed for his conversion because of her belief that a child of many prayers could never be lost. He lost his father at the age of eighteen. He became the bishop of Hippo in Africa and later became one of the greatest interpreters of the scriptures.

Cyril of Alexandria

Cyril was a bishop of Alexandria and was also vast in Scriptural interpretation. He later succeeded his uncle who was a local Patriarch. He discussed scriptural passages with "pathos." He commented on the books of the Bible verse by verse, especially the books of Isaiah, Psalms, John, and Matthew. His acceptance of the books also helped in the process of the formation of the Christian Scripture.

The undisputed truth is that Africa retained its pioneering role of well-established rhetorical tradition during the 2nd and 3rd centuries of the Christian era. The early Christian church was forced to draw up a list of authoritative and acceptable books of the Bible. Upon this basis, the Christian church accepted the present books of the protestant Bible as canonical and authoritative books.

What is most interesting is that most of these African biblical scholars and theologians of the early church have their own canon and the list of the books of the New Testament they accepted as authoritative. Origen, Athanasius, were few examples of people with clear list of acceptable books.[19] Apart from individual list, one of the most important documents for the study of the early history of the canon of the New Testament, Murtorian Canon, was found in the monastery of Bobo in Africa. The first council that accepted the present canon of the books of the New Testament took place in Africa that is in the Synod of Hippo Regius in North Africa.

This section is just a preliminary study of the role and the contribution of Africa and Africans in the formation process of the canon of the New Testament. More research is needed because many western scholars present most of these men and women as western scholars instead of African scholars.

Endnotes

1. Aziz S Atiya, *A Jostpru of Easterm Christianity* (London: Methuen and Co., Ltd. 1986), 13-48. See also his book, *The Copts and Christian Civilization* (Salt Lake City: University of Utah Press, 1979).
2. Ibid. 228.
3. Ibid.,
4. The Association of Mark and Barnabas with Egyptian Christianity, *The Evangelical Quarterly*, 230.
5. Ibid. 231
6. Ibid.
7. Ibid.
8. H.C Snape, "The Fourth Gospel, Ephesus, and Alexandria," 9.
9. H.C Snape, "The Fourth Gospel, Ephesus, and Alexandria," 9.
10. Ibid. 11
11. Some Eurocentric New Testament scholars tried to make him a native of Sicily without any clear evidence. I see that as a continous attempt to give African contribution to someone else.
12. F.F Bruce, *The Canon of the New Testament: It s Origin, Development and Significance* (Oxford: Clarendon Press, 1997), 131
13. F.F Bruce, *The Canon of the New Testament* (Oxford: Claredon Press, 1997), 157
14. Ibid.
15. Donald K. McKim, *Historical Handbook of Major Biblical Interpreters* (Downer Groves: Intervarsity Press, 1998), 8
16. Ibid.161
17. Ibid. 162.
18. Donald K McKim, Ed. *Historical Handbook of Major Biblical Interpreters* (Downers Grove, Intervarsity Press, 1998), 17-21.
19. F.F Bruce, *The Canon of the New Testament*, 305-315

CHAPTER III

TERMS USED TO REFER TO AFRICA AND AFRICANS IN THE NEW TESTAMENT

The term "Africa" does not appear in either the Old or New Testament. The word "Africa," comes from the Greek word *Aphrike* meaning "sunny," or "without cold" and was chiefly applied to the Northern coast of the African continent regarded as an extension of European land.[1] The Latin equivalent of Africa is *Aprica* that also means "sunny." Africa is also a transliteration of the Arabic word *"Ifriqiyah."* One important fact that needs to be known is that the massive land called "Africa" by everyone today has not always been called so. The oldest and the most indigenous name for that massive land is '*Akebu-Lan* or Garden of Eden,' meaning 'Mother of Mankind'.[2] The Ethiopians, Carthaginians, Moors, Nubians, and Namibians used this name.[3] "Kemet, Libya, Ortegia, Corphye, Egypt, Ethiopia and /or Sudan, Olympia, Hesperia, Oceania, Ta-Merry,"[4] Wawat, Cush, Punt or Phut, Nehesi, Magan, and Meluhha are other names used to refer to Africa.

Originally, the Greeks used the word "Libya" to refer to a limited part of the northern part of Africa. In antiquity it refers to that portion opposite the coast of Greece and West of Egypt. The ancient Greeks used the word Ethiopia to refer to the entire continent of Africa (there will be further discussion on this later).

The colonial masters, applied this term to the continent during the partition of Africa instead of using it to avoid having to call the people they captured, chained, and enslaved, their original biblical name such as Akebu-Land, Cush, Ethiopian.

The Greeks, the Romans, and the Jews of the New Testament had contact with the various people of Africa and described them. The New Testament used the terms, Egypt (*Aguptuz*), Libya (*Aibuhz*), Ethiopia (*Aiqiof*), Niger (*Niger*).

Egypt

Egypt as (*Mitzrayim* in Hebrew), along with the cognates was mentioned seven hundred and forty (740) times in the Old Testament. *Cush* or Ethiopia appears fifty-eight (58) times in the Old Testament. In the King James Version, *Cush* was translated as Ethiopia thirty-nine (39) times and was transliterated nineteen times in the Old Testament. It means that the land of Africa and her people were mentioned seven hundred and ninety eight times (798) in the Old Testament. There is no nation or continent that has been mentioned so repeatedly like that of African nations. The implication of this is that, the history of ancient Israel is closely tied with the history of the Black people and Africa. It appears to me that the history of ancient Israel cannot be understood or at least will be incomplete without African nations. No wonder, a scholar concludes "No other land is mentioned so frequently as Egypt in the Old Testament . . . . To understand Israel one must look well to Egypt."[5] The word "Egypt," was once used to refer to the entire continent of the present Africa and its northern part. It was referred to as the "Land of Ham" (Psalm 105). Many ancient historians, such as Diodorus Cicilus, Plutarch, Flavious Josephus, Celsus, Tacitus, and Eusebius, believe that the original Hebrews were some Ethiopians and Egyptians who were forced to Migrate to Canaan.[6] This certainly makes sense because of the biblical account which reports that seventy souls (Gen. 46:27) came to Egypt and lived there for three hundred and thirty years (Ex 12:40). If the Hebrew clan were white by the time they entered Egypt and stayed there for 430 years with the policy of intermarriage in Africa, they would probably have been considerably black by the time they left Egypt.[7] Exodus 12:38 reports that those who left Egypt with the Hebrews were mixed multitudes By the time they left Egypt, they were six hundred thousands souls (Ex. 12:37). Later Egypt was used to refer to a limited portion of the present continent. This word was used in the New Testament to refer to part of Africa and some Africans.

Ethiopians

Scholars owe the origin and the development of the term "Ethiopia" to the ancient Greek writers. Contrary to the prevailing view that the earliest appearance of this term was in the Homeric poem (*Iliad* and *Odyssey*) dating back to the ninth century B.C.E,[8] there is evidence that the first appearance dated back to the second half of the thirteenth century B.C.E. This earliest appearance is in the fragmentary tablets uncovered in the Palace of Nestor at Pylos. Accompanied by frescoes depicting blacks, the word *ai-ti-jo-go* (which was translated to mean aithiops) appeared several times.

During the post-Homeric era, the term Ethiopia became a common expression for the Greco-Roman poets,[9] historians,[10] geographers,[11] and naturalists.[12] Professor Hansberry says that except Hellas and Hellas' own heroes, no country and its peoples are more repeatedly mentioned throughout the long and brilliant course of classical literature.[13] This pride of place given to Ethiopia and Ethiopians by the Greco-Roman geographers, historians, and romanticists shows that these writers were definitely "Ethiopic conscious."[14]

Many theories concerning the etymology of the term "Ethiopia" have been put forward. One of the classical writers say that *Aethiops* which means "glowing" or "black" was the original name of Zeus as he was worshipped in the Island of Chios.[15] But Pliny, the Elder says that the term "Ethiopia" derived from *Aethiops*, the son of Vulcan, who was the god of metalworking and fire and the Greek counterpart of the Ethiopian god of Bes.[16] Professor Edward Glaser maintains that the name *Etiopyawan* (Ethiopia) derived from the word "incense," the frankincense so highly prized in ancient times.[17] However, the scholars' consensus is that the word "Ethiopia" originated from the Greeks to designate African people both at home and abroad in terms of the color of their skins. This term which the Greek geographers generally used to refer to the black people derived from the words (burnt) and (face[18]). Ethiopia, therefore, literally means "burnt-faced person" of Africa and African Diaspora. This term was probably chosen by the Greeks to describe the Africans according to their "environmental theory" that the dark colour of their skins and the wooly or coiled hair of their heads were as a result of the "intense heat of the southern sun."

According to the Homeric testimony, the land of Ethiopia is at the remotest border of the world beside the steam of the ocean. It was the place where the "blameless race of men" called Ethiopians lived. They made sacrifices pleasing to the gods, including Zeus.[19] Two Ethiopians exist, the Ethiopia of the rising and the setting sun.[20]

The exact meaning of the Ethiopians of the rising and setting suns has been the subject of debate even among the Homeric scholars. While some scholars say that the two divisions of Ethiopia mean that one Ethiopia is Africa and the other Asia, other scholars interpret it to mean that Ethiopia south of Egypt was divided by River Nile.[21] Hesiod lists Ethiopians with the Ligurians and Scythians as quoted by Strabo.[22] In the Theogony, Memnon, the son of Eos is the King of Ethiopia. In the *Work and Days*, Hesiod referred to the Ethiopians for the first time as black men.[23]

Aeschylus is the first Greek writer to place Ethiopians definitely in Africa when he refers to the dark race as Ethiopians who dwell near the Ethiopian river (Nile) the spring of the sun where the Ethiopian river (Nile) is located. Hanno's voyage is described as one of the "most picturesque incidents" in the history of ancient geography.[24] "Unfortunately, the name Hanno was so common in Carthage and that makes it difficult to identify which Hanno. However, generally, scholars date it between sixth and fifth centuries B.C.E[25]. Although scholars doubt the southern limit of Hanno's voyage (because the places mentioned have not been located), Hanno seems to have been the first to describe a voyage to the most southern part of Africa for the purpose of colonization. Hanno sailed as far as river Lixus, where the natives told him about the high mountains and the hostile Ethiopians who were cave-dwellers in inner Africa[26] They sailed beyond Cerne into a great lake where wild people threw stones at them, thus preventing them from landing. The report said that they sailed to a large river full of "crocodiles and hippopotami" (this river is generally identified with Senegal).[27] They went further to a bay, generally identified with Gambia in West Africa. Beyond this bay, was the great gulf called Western Horn. Sailing beyond the Western Horn, they arrived at a bay called the Southern Horn where they saw an island full of people covered with hair and called "gorillas." This was the southern limit of their expedition.[28]

A man who, in the west, earned the title "Father of History" (given by Cicero), and "the first artist of Greek prose" is Herodotus. His travels to Persia, Palestine, Europe, and Egypt for inspection of ruins of the ancient fallen civilization in order to determine differences among nations resulted in his book Histories. Of interest to scholars is the signature of Herodotus that was uncovered at Asmara, Northern Ethiopia.[29] However, some scholars consider this signature a spurious one. Despite the fact that the ancient Greek geographer, Strabo, called him the "compiler of lies," and some modern scholars distrusted his work, archaeological discoveries appear to authenticate his records, especially concerning Africa (Book II and III). Herodotus, like Homer, mentioned two types of Ethiopians in the army of Xerxes which invaded Greece in 480 B.C.E (Western and Eastern Ethiopians).[30] Budge interprets Herodotus as saying that the classical historians and geographers knew the "whole region from India to Egypt" by name Ethiopia. They regarded all the dark skinned and black people who lived in that vast region as Ethiopians.[31]

"The Father of History" did not just generalize the Western and the Eastern Ethiopians without making some valuable distinctions. According to him, both were black, but the hair of the Western Ethiopians was coiled and woolly while the hair of the Eastern Ethiopians was straighter and there were differences in the languages they spoke.[32] Herodotus, who spent about two years in Egypt for his research, regarded the Egyptians and the Colchians as black people. He says: There can be no doubt that Colchains are an Egyptian race. Before I heard any mention of the fact from others, I had remarked it myself. My own conjectures were founded first on the fact that they are black skinned and have wooly hair.[33]

The Ethiopians in the army of Xerxes wore leopard and lion skins, and were armed with spears, bows and arrows.[34] In order to prove that the ocean surrounded Africa, Herodotus further reports what took place during the reign of

Pharaoh Necho. The Phoenicians, he says, circumnavigated Africa in the period of three years and returned through the Pillar of Hercules.[35] He believes this incident but rejects the idea that the sun was on their right hand during the expedition. He also relates another abortive attempt to circumnavigate Africa by the Persian noble man, Sataspes, who was sentenced to death unless he circumnavigated Africa (Ethiopia).[36] He failed and was executed. E. H. Brunbury agrees that the above incident cannot be disproved or pronounced impossible.[37] Other statements about Ethiopia and Ethiopians which are of historical value are: Shabaka's invasion of Egypt, Psammetichus' employment of the Greek mercenaries against his southern neighbours.[38] Cambyses' plan to attack them and his failure[177], their longevity,[39] and their heights and good looks ("the tallest and handsomest men in the whole world").[40] Additional interesting material which is of major importance concerning the Ethiopians was given by Eudoxus of Cyzicus, and was preserved by Strabo[41] was sent on an honorary mission to sail around Ethiopia. During his voyage he saw the Ethiopians (West) who spoke the same language as those of the Eastern Ethiopians and there he learned that their territory adjoined that of Brocchus, King of Mauretania.[42] He went beyond his Mauretania and then reported that Ethiopia was surrounded by the ocean.[43]

An unknown author in his work Periplus of the Erythrean gave another interesting account about Ethiopia. He was regarded as the first person to show a definite knowledge of the southern extension of Africa among the Greek writers. Some of the places mentioned are identifiable with reasonable certainty He sailed south of Aromata as far as Zanzibar, Rhapta, and further to about 1,500 miles south of Cape Guardafui.[44]

Diodorus Sicilus (59-30 B.C.E.), the Greek-born writer, set out to write the general history of mankind. Although charged with lack of methodology of his plan, and deficiency in his critical judgment as to his selection and use of materials, modern scholars believe that his work is one of the most trustworthy and valuable, especially the section which deals with Ethiopia.[45] Although he says that some Ethiopians were primitive,[46] he was not blind to the achievement of the Ethiopians. According to Diodorus Sicilus the Ethiopians were people of great wisdom and religious zeal. These are the inhabitants of the Island of Meroe, according to his sources, were the first of all men; they were pioneers in the worship of God; they originated many Egyptian customs; they were the people who sent the Egyptians out as colonists; they originated the Egyptian burial practices, the role of priests, the shape of statues and their forms of writing.[47] According to Diodorus, the stories about Osiris of Egypt and Dionysus of the Greeks were nothing but the "glorified editions of events and exploits which were originally performed by the prince who belong to the old royal family of inner Ethiopia[48] Diodorus mentioned the king of Ethiopia, Sabach, who invaded Egypt, as noted for kindness and zeal more than his predecessors."[49] To him the reason why the people beyond Egypt were different in life, manners and bodies is because of the intense heat of that region. Strabo, who is one of the most remarkable scholars of antiquity, earned himself the appellation "the Father of Geography," mainly because of his monumental work, Geography. Although his first efforts in the field of "productive scholarship" were in history, his book on geography is by far the most important geographical work ever produced by the Greco-Roman writers that have come down from antiquity. Alexander van Hamboldt's statement on Strabo's geography is that this work surpassed all other geographical labours of antiquity by the grandeur of its composition and diversity of its subjects, Hansberry believes that this is not an overstatement.[50]

Unfortunately, this seventeenth book, which is said to be the most "complete and satisfactory portion of Strabo's entire work," is the one that deals with Ethiopia. Strabo, like Diodorus, mentioned the power of the priests to punish even the king of the country and one king who abolished this type of power accorded to the priests in Ethiopia. In their religion, says Strabo[51] the Ethiopians honored one being as God who is regarded as immortal and caused the existence of all things. In addition to the people of Meroe, Strabo mentioned the Egyptian fugitives who deserted their king Psameticus and dwelled beyond Meroe. He called this people "Sembutae." According to him the Nubae (probably the Nubia) lived at the left bank of the Nile. Other groups include Megari and Blemmyes. Some of the historical events about the Roman invasion of Meroe when the Ethiopians seized the statues of Caesar were said to have been authenticated by archaeological discoveries. Such a statue was reported to have been uncovered in 1914 by the Liverpool Expedition who, when they excavated Meroe, uncovered a bronze head which appeared to be a portrait of Caesar.[52] G. A. Reisner of the Harvard-Boston Expedition who excavated the ruins of the great Temple of Ethiopia, near Nepata, claimed to have uncovered what he regards as evidence of the damages done by the Romans.[53]

Pliny the Elder is very important because his work is one of the most important of the Latin writers. Among his contemporaries, he was regarded as one of the "most learned," most diligent and most voluminous writers of the ancient times. Of all the books he wrote, only the *Natural History* survived. This work contains the most numerous references to Ethiopia. This might be because he was able to consult other classical writers before him. According to Pliny, the region designated as Ethiopia in ancient times had different names. The earliest of these names is Aetherea, then, Altantia, and last Aethiopia, which he said derived from Aethiops, the son of Vulcan, the Latin name of the god of the metalworking and fire.[54] Pliny was more detailed and more specific about the cities of Ethiopia. Pliny says that the Egyptians who deserted Psammetichus settled in the cities five days journey beyond Meroe. Another eight days journey further south was another city called Nubae. Beyond Nubae, says Pliny, were scattered towns like Asara, Araba, and Summara. The people called Cisori, Misyti, who were remarkable for the unerring aim of their arrows, settled beyond these towns mentioned above. Further south were still many other towns-Longompoli, Oecalices, Usibalei, Isbeli, Pemsii and Cespil. Finally, imaginary people inhabited the southern land beyond. Pliny was the first ancient writer to mention the river Niger, which he calls river Nigries.[55] This river, he says, has the same characteristics as the river Nile. It produces reeds, papyrus which becomes swollen at the same time. The question of identification of the river Nigris of Pliny to the River Niger in West Africa is still debatable. However, Professor Bunbury says that in the absence of any river in the north of the great desert which fits the description of river Nigris, it must refer to the inner African river known in the modern times as river Niger.[56]

Although these cities have not been identified with certainty, the fact that these ancient writers mentioned them is remarkable and gives some indication that the nation called Ethiopia is not confined to the area of Meroe and probably includes all the territory of modern Africa. This appears very probable when one examines the reports of Herodotus and Eudoxus of Cynicus. Herodotus reported that the Phoenicians circumnavigated Ethiopia. Euxodus went beyond Mauritania and reported that Ethiopia was surrounded by the ocean. From the above discussion of the term Ethiopia during the classical period, it appears that it is reasonably certain that these classical writers were well acquainted with and well informed about Ethiopia and Ethiopians. It also appears reasonably certain that the term "Ethiopia" and "Ethiopians" were first used in a more general sense (especially in the time of Homer, Hesiod and Herodotus) to refer to all dark-skinned people and all the land which they inhabited. (Egypt, Sudan, Arabia, Palestine, Western Asia and India), but more frequently to African people and their land. The use of Ethiopia in this way probably roughly corresponds to *Cush, Punt*, and *Nehesi* of the Egyptians, Assyrians and Hebrews.

When the *King James Version* of the Bible was translated, the word "*Kush*" was translated as "Ethiopia," thus transliterating the Septuagint (LXX). In 1901, the revision done by the "American divines," *The American Standard Version*, retained the term "Ethiopian." The same term is used in the *Revised Standard Version* of 1952, which set out to make the Bible clearer to the public reader by changing some of the archaic words. *The New American Standard Version* of 1960 used this same term in some of its passages. *The Jerusalem Bible* and *The New International* Version used the transliteration of the Hebrew word (*Kush*). *The Good News Bible*, which translates *Kush* as "Sudan," seems to have a better translation even though it is equally an unsatisfactory translation like others mentioned above.

Although the word "Sudan" means "black," it is deficient because it still excludes some parts of Africa represented by the biblical *Kush*. On this account, the Alfred the author of *The Black Man in the Old Testament and Its World*, laments that the translation of the term Kush as "Ethiopia" is "a definite disservice to the Christian Church in general, and to the black African and his descendants in particular," because the translation of this term as Ethiopia obscures the role the black people have played in the Bible. This obscurity of the role of blacks in the Bible might have contributed in some ways to the "continuing scourge of slavery that mars the pages of Western history," because the Western conscience might possibly have reacted differently had the biblical Ethiopians been more closely identified. In other words, the subsequent generation might have been protected from the "color disease" if a different translation which reflected black people had been employed.[57]

What this writer thinks should be the most appropriate translation of *Cush* according to the principle of translation discussed above is "Africa," or "Black." So also in every passage where the word "Ethiopian," and "Niger," occur in the New Testament should be translated "African," or "Black."[58] This term "Africa" is the most natural equivalent of the biblical term today. This term will not only convey the black identity of the people referred to as *Kush*, but it would also likely not to be misunderstood by the common English readers.

Alexandria

Ya'kub Nakhabah Bey Fufilah who is a native Egyptian wrote a book titled *History of Copts* in 1899 and stated, "The appearance of the Christian faith and its introduction into our country in the middle of the 1st century after the birth of Christ came about through the preaching of St. Mark the Evangelist, whose preaching was followed by the conversion of multitudes of the people." In contrast to the above statement, the majority of modern Eurocentric scholars consistently attempt to disprove such ideas without any valid evidence. One such scholar is Scott Moncrieff who contended that when and how Christianity came to Egypt is unknown and that the tradition that makes St. Mark the preacher of the gospel in Alexandria has no foundation.[59] It is an indisputable fact that early in the second half of the 1st century some knowledge of the Christian faith had reached Egypt. There is evidence that by 180CE when Christianity flourished in Alexandria there were other flourishing institutions with an organization and school of higher learning attached which had made its influence felt beyond the city itself.

We are sure that the city of Alexandria in Africa was one of the chief cities of Egypt and one of the most important cities of the ancient world. It was most noted for the exportation of grains to other ancient cities of the empire. Though it numbered among her population Greeks and Jewish, it will be unthinkable to say that there were not many, if not more Egyptian natives. It will be certainly strange to believe that there were no native Africans in Alexandria considering the policy of Alexander, the Great. He encouraged all his military men to intermarry in order to unify the world under one Hellenistic policy and culture. In Alexandria was a famous port noted for its export of grain to most of the Mediterranean world. In fact, it was the greatest port in the eastern Mediterranean to which people constantly sailed. It is relatively certain that Jews of Alexandria must also have gone to Jerusalem quite often. As famous as the city of Alexandria was in Africa in the ancient world, it will make no sense to think that Christianity had not come to that city very early in the year. They would probably have come to the city in two ways: by way of the Gentile converts to the Greek citizen and the Jewish Christian church in Jerusalem to the Jewish community in Alexandrian city. We know that Christianity made its early converts in synagogues among the Jews and Gentiles. "God fearers" who attended the synagogues were sympathetic with the Jews. In this case the large presence of Jews in Egypt, especially the Delta and Alexandria, made it very likely that Christianity originated from Africa-Egypt. We are certain that the Jews have been present in Egypt from the days of Jeremiah (Jer. 44:4). Even before then Africa as a whole (*Cush*) had a very strong relationship with the people of Israel from time immemorial, especially from the time of Abraham. Interaction among them was strong. The political and economic opportunity in Egypt favoured this strong relation. There was therefore political, religious, economic, and military relationship.[60] During the early pre-Christian centuries they settled throughout the country. There were synagogues in each section of the city of Alexandria in the time of Philo. Two of the city's sections were regarded as Jewish. Philo gave the figure of the Jewish to be one million. Diodorus Siculus estimated the population of Egypt to be seven million in the time of Ptolemy, but Josephus (War ii 16:4) believed that it was seven and half million excluding Alexandria. The fact is that the Jewish population was indeed high enough to attract the early Christian missionaries. It is, therefore, unlikely that the missionaries could have ignored such a large population of the "chosen people." Perhaps, Mark was there to preach to this large Jewish population. The failure of Paul to preach in Egypt is in accordance to his principle "to preach the Gospel, not where Christ has already been named, lest he build on another man's foundation" (Rom. 15:20; cf. 2 Cor. 10:13, 15-16).[61] It is important to remember that the great and eloquent teacher Apollos in the Acts of the Apostles 18 and also in Paul's First Epistle to the Corinthians came from Alexandria.[62] It is also significant to mention that the famous Codez Bezae, and uncial, and Bilingual manuscripts of the New Testament (now in Cambridge) mentioned that Apollos received his instruction "in way of the Lord" from Alexandria, his native African city.[63] The famous 4th century historian, Eusebius, mentioned the tradition that Mark preached the Gospel in Alexandria. He further mentioned that Mark appointed his successor, Annianos, over the church of Alexandria during the 8th year of Nero (61-62CE). Jerome, the translator of the Vulgate version of the Bible was not silent concerning Mark's activities in Alexandria. He mentioned that Mark was martyred in Alexandria and that his corpse was buried there. It has been long believed that such is the reason why the church in Alexandria was dedicated to the Saint. Although Clement and Origen did not mention the tradition of the presence of St. Mark in Alexandria that did suggest that it never happened. They probably took for granted that such tradition was well known and widely believed. It was, therefore, not necessary to repeat what is generally believed and well known that time.

From the above, is it not likely that Christianity originated from Africa, namely Egypt? First, it might be as a result of the large presence of the Jews in Egypt. It is remarkable that the earliest New Testament fragment consisting of John 18:31-33, 37, 38 was found in Egypt.

The early presence of Gnosticism in Egypt is important evidence that Christianity came very early to Egypt. Perhaps, it is important to explain what

Gnosticism is. It is actually a version of Christianity. It came up as a result of the preaching of the Christian Gospel. It emphasized that the message of the Gospel was two fold. First, to those simple Christians who only needed guidance in life? Second, to the actual initiates who were enlightened and worthy of understanding of deep mysteries? It can be considered the adaptation of the Christian Gospel to the need of those Christians who wanted better or higher spiritual apprehension (*gnosis*) than the ordinary people. It promised the devotee purity from sin and the possibility of obtaining immortality. Africa, especially Egypt, which has been the home of mystery and magic, became a favorable place for Gnostic teachings. It made a wide appeal to the people who desired further knowledge of secrets, powers and occult like authority. There is clear evidence of Gnosticism in Egypt as early as the middle of the second century C.E. We know of at least two leading Gnostists from Egypt, namely, Basilides and Valentinus. Basilides was active in the reign of Hadrian. Valentinus was born in Arsinoe and was said to have been originally a Christian whose speculation led to the embrace Gnosticism. The early presence of Gnosticism was evidence that Christianity was in Egypt very early.

The presence of the famous Catechetical School of Alexandria which had produced, by the end of the 2nd century CE, famous African theologians and teachers such as Clement and Origen is an evidence that Christianity reached Alexandria very early. Clement, who was converted to Christianity as a young man, came to Alexandria under the influence of Pantaenus, his predecessor as head of the famous Catechetical School in Alexandria. He brought a wealth of Greek learning to Alexandria. Origen (185-254), Clement's pupil, could possibly be regarded as the boldest thinker in the whole history of Christendom. It was in his writing that we first found reference to the Egyptians as Christians as opposed to Greeks. Eusebius also mentioned in his history that Christians from Egypt were brought to Alexandria to be martyred.

The persecution of Diocletian was mostly directed to the champion of faith from Egypt whether they were Copts or Roman by birth. He "attacked the Christians, slew them, destroyed their churches, inflicted punishments upon their leaders, and made slaves of their women and children."[64] It should be remembered that the great movement called Monasticism is purely African in origin. The most famous, and the founder of the ascetic movement was St. Anthony (251-354CE) who was an Egyptian.

The great heretic, Arius, a priest of Alexandria, who maintained that God created Christ was from Alexandrian. Even though he was the highest and most eminent of all creations of God, he was not God in the sense that God the Father is God. It is also remarkable that the champion of Orthodox Christianity was an African (Egyptian) in the person of "the indomitable Athanasius." He defended orthodox Christianity against Arius' heresy.

Libya

Libya (*Libuhz*) is one of the terms used in the New Testament to refer to Africa and Africans. Some scholars believe that this term is translated from three distinctive Hebrew words: *Kub*, *Lubim*, and *Lehabim*. In Genesis 10:13 the word Lehabim is mentioned. The Old Testament references to Libya links it with Egyptians and Ethiopians (II Chron. 12:3; 16:8; Ezek. 30:5; Dan. 11:5; Dan. 11:13; Nahum 3:9). The New Testament also links Egypt with Libya. Josephus says that there were many Jews who lived in Libya and that Cyreneans consisted of native citizens, husbandmen, strangers and Jews.[65]

While the Greek and Roman historians and poet used the word *Libyes* to refer to the inhabitants of North Africa, others like Herodotus and Sallust used the term Libya to refer to the entire continent of Africa. However, Strabo sometimes used it to refer to only a limited area of North Africa.[66] Diodorus used Libya to refer to Africa of the Nile as far as Egypt is concerned.[67]

Cyrene

Cyrene (*Kurene*) was the chief city of the ancient district of North Africa called Cyrenaica. It later became the capital city of Cyrenaica in North Africa where the present Libya is located. The city was also called Pentapolis. It was said to have been founded in 630 BCE, by Dorian Greeks from the Islands of Thera and Crete.[68] Eventually the Peloponnesian settlers joined the city. The city became very important because of agriculture and its trade with the natives of the interior. The land was very fertile especially for the production of silphium. They were good in agricultural product used for the production of silphium (a plant in high demand for spices and medicine) on which their wealth depended. This plant became a badge for their coins. The five cities of Pentapolis or Cyrenaica enjoyed great prosperity until the competition from the Ptolemaic cities, the internal disruptions and careless use of the soil caused their decline. A city of about 100,000 later declined by the fifth century CE. Eventually, the prosperity of Cyrene declined because of too much exploitation of the land. The silphium supply was finally exhausted during the time of Nero.

It appears that the settlers dominated the natives and Battiade ruled the city until the establishment of her democracy in the fourth century BCE. By the fourth century BCE. the city of Cyrene had a democratic government and had established a philosophical school.[69] This city eventually was taken by Alexander, the Great in 331 and later became part of the Ptolemy's kingdom. In 96 BCE, it became a Roman city and was later united with Crete. During this period, the city also had many Greek-speaking people who were mainly Jews who sent by Ptolemies of Egypt. They enjoyed equal right with the entire population including the natives.

Cyrene was an important intellectual and medical center in antiquity. Some of the famous citizens include a poet, Callimachus, Carneades, the founder of the New Academy at Athens, and Erostasthenes, the historian. Aristippus, was the name of the founder of the Cyreniac Greek school of Greek philosophy. This is one of the earliest Socratic schools, which emphasized one aspect of Socratic teaching that happiness, or pleasure is the highest good.

A number of Cyrenians were mentioned in many events recorded in the New Testament. These people include Simon, who helped carry the cross of Christ to Golgotha (Matt. 27:32, Mark 15:21). Lucius was one of the prophets and teachers of the primitive church in Antioch (Acts 13:1). Stephen who was stoned to death in the synagogue to which Cyrenians and Alexandrians were prominent members (Acts 6:9) was probably an Alexandrian. Foreign men who were included in the membership of this synagogue were men of Cyrene, Alexandria, Cilicia, and Asia. The truth is that Cyrenians and Alexandrians convert to Jewry, who took Jewish citizenship, were prominent people among the Jews in Jerusalem and elsewhere abroad (Acts.2: 10). These people were probably native Africans sent by Ptolemies to settle in Alexandria and Cyrene. Under Vespasian the Jews revolted and that had a devastating effect on the people of Cyrene. In 115-116, pagan monuments that were erected, burnt and smashed, over 200,000 inhabitants were murdered.

In the nineteenth century the monuments were explored, first by the Americans (1910-1911), and later by the Italians just before the Second World War II. They found the Temple of Apollo which has been rebuilt several times and later transformed into the Christian church in the fourth century CE. They also found many other temples and buildings for the cult of Roman emperors, such as baths, and a theater.[70]

Niger (Niger)

The word Niger occurs only once in the New Testament, namely, in Acts. 13:1. This word is a Latin word, which means "black."[71] As discussed earlier in my introduction, the Hebrew word *Cush* in the Old Testament means black, and in the LXX it was translated to *Ethiopia* and that also means black. In the New Testament, the words *Ethiopia* and *Niger* were used as the equivalent of the Old Testament word *Cush*.[72] In the experience of the Romans, Ethiopians were not the only people with flat noses, thick lips, tightly coiled hair, which the Romans describe as Niger, Roman literature described swarthy, or dark skinned people as Niger among the various terms employed. The people in this category are Africans including the Egyptians, Libyans, Moors, some Indians and certain persons of mixed parentage with black and white. The truth is that the Greek words commonly used to describe the Ethiopians' color in the classical period was melas (melaz) and its compounds, in Latin, the adjective most frequently used for the Ethiopians who are of black skinned is *niger* as equivalence of Ethiopia (Aiqioy).[73]

The legendary Ethiopian king called Memnon (600 BCE) who fought in the Trojan War at Troy was referred to sometimes as Memnon *aethiops*, and other times as Memnon *Niger*.[74]

So also in the New Testament, the Greek word Niger was transliterated "Niger" respectively by *The King James Version*. The *Revised Standard Version* transliterated it "Niger", The *American Standard Version* and *the New International, Jerusalem Bible Versions* also transliterated it "Niger." *The Good News Bible, The New American Standard Version, The Living Bible* and the *New Living Translation*, translated it "the black person." This is highly commendable.

The transliteration of the word "Niger" to Niger is also a disservice to all the black people all over the world. The meaning of the word Niger in Greek and Latin in the New Testament should be translated "African" or "Black" instead of the present transliteration to Niger. It certainly obscures the identity and the role of the black people in the drama of redemption. As said above, *The Good News Bible, The American Standard Version*, and *The Living Bible* did a very commendable job by translating the word "Niger" to "the black person."

Endnotes

1. "Africa," *The New Encyclopedia Britannica*, Vol. I, 15th edition (William Benton, 1973),
2. Cain Hope Felder, (General Editor), *The Original African Heritage Study Bible* (Nashville: Wiston-Derek Publishers, Inc. 1998), 102
3. Ibid.
4. Ibid., 102-103
5. John Paterson, "The Old Testament World, " in *The Bible and History*, ed. by William Barclay (Nashville and New York: Abingdon Press, 1968), 39. See also Charles Copher, *Black Biblical Studies* (Chicago: Black Light Fellowship, 1993), 45, 58.
6. Ibid. 103
7. Ibid.102.
8. Frank M. Snowden, Jr., *The Image of the Black*, Vol. 1. *Before Color Prejudice: Ancient View of the Blacks* (Cambridge: Harvard University Press, 1983. According to Snowden, the population of early Crete probably included many black African people. This is can be attested to by the Archaeological discoveries. A fragmentary fresco discovered at Thera in 1968 shows a black man with thick lip. This was dated to 1350-1500 BCE. At the palace of Nestor at Pylos, another fresco was found depicting another black man dating back to the thirteen century BCE. These finding dating to the early period in Greece shows that the Greeks have been familiar with Africans from the early period and that their testimonies about Africans are authentic. See pages 136-138.
9. Some of these poets are Hesiod, Aeschylus, Apollonius, Quintus, Arctinus of Miletus. See William Leo Hansberry, *Africa and Africans as seen by the Classical Writers* (Washington DC: Howard University Press, 1977), 5.

    Some of these poets are Hesiod, Aeschylus, Apollonius, Quintus, Arctinus of Miletus. See William Leo Hansberry, *Africa and Africans as seen by the Classical Writers* (Washington DC: Howard University Press, 1977), 5.
10. These historians are Herodotus and Diodorus. Ibid, 5.
11. Some of these geographers include Hecateaus, Ephorus, Eratosthenes, Agatharchides and Strabo, Ibid. 5.
12. The naturalist includes Pliny, Callisthenies and Heliodorus. Ibid. 5.
13. Ibid. 20.
14. Ibid. , 5.
15. Pliny, vi:187.80.
16. Ibid.
17. Sylvia Pankhurst, (Essex: House, 1959), *Ethiopia A Cultural History* (Essex: House, 1959), 10.

18. They were called so because of their understanding that the people of Africa were black because of their closeness to the sun which burnt their bodies.
19. Homer, *Iliad,* 1.423-24, 23,.205-7
20. *Odyssey*, 1.22-24; 4.84,5.282; Hansberry, 74-75
21. Hansberry, 102
22. Hesiod, Theogony, 984-85
23. Hesiod, *Work and Days*, 527
24. Harry Burton, *The Discovery of Ancient World* (Cambridge: Harvard University Press, 1932),29
25. Ibid.
26. Ibid,. 32.
27. Ibid.,81.
28. Ibid., 81.
29. Alfred Haddon, *History of Anthropology* (London: Watts & Co, 1934), 1
30. Herodotus, VII.70.
31. Wallis Budge, *History of Ethiopia: Nubia and Abyssinia* vol. 1 (London: Methuen and Company, 1928), vii-viii. Herodotus is probably justified in calling the black inhabitants of Asia Ethiopians not only because of their black color, but also because their various traditions, culture and religious practices which link their origin with Africa.
32. Herodotus, VII, 70
33. Ibid., Book II, 114-115
34. Ibid., VII, 69
35. Ibid., IV, 42
36. Ibid., 43
37. E.H Bunbury, *A History of Ancient Geography*, vol. I (New York: Dover Publication, 1959), 296.
38. Herodotus, II, 2:137-40; 2:152-54. Names of the missionaries who participated in this expedition of Nubia appeared in the inscriptions discovered in
    Abu Simbel. See *Image of the Black,* 39
    39. Ibid., II.14,20-23
    40. Ibid.
41 Strabo, II.3
42. Bunbury, *A History of Ancient Geography*, vol 2, 74-77
43. Ibid.
44. Ibid., 91
45. Hansberry, *Africa and Africans*, 115
46. Diodorus, 3.8.5, 3.25.2, 3.9.2
47. Hansberry, 118
48. Diodorus, 3.11., 3.2-3.7
49. Hansberry, 123
50. Hansberry, 124
51. Strabo, 17.3

52. Hansberry, 180
53. Ibid. 133
54. Ibid. 139-40
55. Pliny 5.8.46, 6.35, 188
56. *A History of Ancient Geography*, vol. 2, 436.
57. Edward Dunston, *The Black Man in the Old Testament and Its World* (Philadelphia: Dorrance & Co, 1974), 18
58. Africa has been used as names of people. For example, Africanus.
59. See J.M. Plumley, "Early Christianity in Egypt," *Palestine Exploration Quarterly*, 89 (1957), 70-81.
60. See my book, Africa and the Africans in the Old Testament.
61. Perhaps, the silence of Luke the evangelist may be due to two main reasons: he was not really interested writing the world history of Christianity; he was mainly interested in the missionary activities of Paul his friend who concentrated his activities between Jerusalem and Rome. It was along this road that Luke was interested in relating the progress of Christianity. This northward area is where he knew best. His seeming neglect of Egyptian Christianity does not mean that Christianity was absent in Egypt during the early years of Christianity.
62. John J. Gunther, "The Association of Mark and Barnabas with Egyptian Christianity," *The Evangelical Qaurterly* 54 (1982):219-233.
63. J. Plumley, "Early Christianity in Egypt," *Palestine Exploration Quarterly* (henceforth PEQ) 89 (1957), 70-81.
64. Ibid., 76
65. Josephus, *Antiquity*, Book XVI chapter VII no 2.
66. C.O.G Ndubukwu, "Some Concepts of the Africa Literature," Unpublished PhD Thesis, University of Ibadan, 1979, 12-14.
67. Joseph E. Harris, *Africa and Africans as seen by Classical Writers* (Washington DC: Howard University Press, 1901)
68. Herodotus IV. 150 ff.
69. M.J. Mellink, "Cyrene," *Interpreter's Dictionary of the Bible* (IDB) George A. Buttrick ed. (Nashville: Abingdon Press, 1986), 754.
70. Ibid.
71. "Niger," Joseph H Thayer, *The New Thayers Greek-English Lexicon of the New Testament* (Lafayette: The Book Factory, 1979).
72. Charles B Copher, *Black Biblical Studies* (Chicago: Black Light Publications, 1997), 98. See also Friday Peter Udoisang, "Africa and Africans in the New Testament," Unpublished M.A Thesis, Delta State University, Abraka, Nigeria, 1998.
73. Frank Snowden, *Blacks in Antiquity. Ethiopians in the Greco Roman Experience* (Cambridge; Harvard University Press, 1970),3. See also Friday P. Udoisang, MA Thesis, Delta State University, Nigeria, 1998.
74. Frank Snowden, *Blacks in Antiquity*, 4. The Garamentes in the North Western part of Africa are referred to as Ethiopians and at times as dark (*Nigri*).

CHAPTER IV

HOW EGYPT BECAME A MELTING POT

At this stage I think that it is important to discuss how Egypt became a melting pot. As early as 2000 BCE Abraham (Gen. 12:20), Joseph, and his family went to Egypt. It was probably during the Middle Kingdom of Egypt and during the Twelfth Dynasty (1991BCE). It was the golden age of Egyptian classical literature and the time when the Egyptians were careful of its Asiatic frontier.[1] There is also a pictorial document in a famous tomb-scene at Benihasan showing the 37 groups of Asiatics visiting Egypt.

During the Second Intermediate Period (2200-1570), the people referred to as Hyksos invaded Egypt. There is no unanimous agreement as to how the Hyksos came to dominate Egypt. One group of scholars believed that they conquered and took Egypt by force, while others believed that they came in peace as friends, settled down, intermarried and later took over Egypt because of Egyptian hospitality like any other African country. At this time there were many Semitic (Asiatics) servants in Egypt as far as Thebes, serving. It was reported that many Semitic chiefs of foreign lands gained prominence in Lower Egypt and then took over the kingship of Egypt at Ithet-Tawy forming the 15th and 16th Hyksos Dynasties of Egypt (1650-1542). After ruling for about 100 years they were later driven away by the native Egyptians under the leadership of Ahmose. Before they were driven away, they took over the administration, and appointed Semitic people into high offices. It was this time that Joseph was in Egypt (Gen.37-50).

During the New Kingdom, in 19th Dynasty (1300-1200), Ramses campaigned against the Hittites (Hattusi III) and finally signed a peace treaty that probably brought many Hittites to Egypt. The Successor of Ramses, Mrenptah also raided Palestine and captured Gezer.[2] This dynasty, was the period of "movements of peoples or large groups." It was reported that there was constant coming and going between the Egyptians and the Canaanites.[3]

In Dynasty 20, under the leadership of Ramses III (1190-1180BCE) there were also great folk-movements in the Eastern Mediterranean basin. This period of Ramses III also witnessed Egypt's last imperial pharaoh.

In Dynasty 21, when King David conquered Edom, Hadad, was taken to Egypt for safety. He was so welcomed that when he grew up he was given a royal Egyptian wife (I Kings 11:18-22). During Dynasty 22, the so-called Bubastic Dynasty, Sheshonq I (Biblical Shishak) had aggressive policy toward the Asiatics and Israel. He worked for the breakdown of the Hebrew Kingdom. He did not attack Israel during the reign of Solomon but harboured many refugees from Israel, notably, Jeroboam, son of Nebat (I King 11:29-40). The return of Jeroboam brought about the break down of the Hebrew Kingdom. Eventually Shishak invaded Palestine and subdued the Kingdoms.[4]

From what has been said above, foreigners have ruled Egypt almost endlessly until the so-called Ethiopian or Cushite Dynasty. That was the time when the native African Pharaohs were able to regain their land that had been taken over by foreigners. Kashta and Piankhy laid claim to Upper Egypt and later Lower Egypt when Piankhy subdued Tafnekht of Lower Egypt. Shabaka (716-702) became his successor and reconquered Egypt after some struggle. Despite all the Shabaka neutral policy toward the Assyrians, his successor had several military engagements with them.[5]

In 664/663, Ashurbanipal, the Assyrian ruler, finally sacked the holy City of Thebes and plunged the temple treasures. The writer of the book of Nahum vividly described the downfall of Thebes by the Assyrians (Nahum 3:8-10). Although the Assyrians could not totally occupy Thebes, they left some key garrisons in Egypt.

Psammeticus I of Egypt managed to establish the 26th Dynasty and built an effective army around "a hard core Greek mercenaries. Greek merchants were also allowed and encouraged to come to Egypt freely.

After the destruction of Jerusalem in 587/6 BCE, Nebuchadrezzer of Babylon marched against the "Black Country," Egypt, and subdued it until some agreement was reached between Egypt and Babylonia. In 525 BC, Egypt followed her allies into Persian dominion under Cambyses. Under Dairus I, Persian rule was fair and tolerant, until Egyptians manufactured anti-Persian propaganda. In about 400-341 BCE Egyptians last native Pharaoh gained some independence (Dynasty 28-30). They were eventually overwhelmed by the Persians to whom they remained a subject for about 9 years until Alexander the Great entered Egypt as a liberator of Egypt from the Persian in 332 BCE. After that Egypt became a Hellenistic monarchy under the Ptolemies.

As from the 3rd century, Egypt was largely a Christian land (Coptic) until 641/2 C.E when Islamic conquest overran Egypt.

The above discussion is an attempt to explain why Egyptians seem to become whiter in color than the normal African people. Beginning from the time of Abraham, the Hyksos, the Assyrians, the Babylonians, the Persians, the Greeks, and the Romans, the Byzantine and the Arabs, have their share in dominating and intermarrying Egyptian people. The evidence is strong as discussed above that Egyptians are Africans and the land of Egypt has been African land. The culture and civilization, no doubt, is African civilization no matter how some western scholars try to remove everything Egyptian from Africa.

Egyptian Depictions in Art

Egyptians depicted themselves in their painting in different ways. Some are black in colour, while others are dark red and reddish-brown.[6] Some people object that these colors are not relevant to the determination whether the Ancient Egyptians were black, simply because of the observation that in some statues women are lighter than men. To such people this different characterization does not reflect the actual reality of the color of ancient Egyptians. According to them these artist may be employing idealized colors for men and women in Ancient Egypt.[7] The above ideas are untenable because in most Egyptian pictures, women are dark-skinned, bright red, dark -brown and others just exactly the way they portrayed men. Usury and Keener agree to the fact that the idea of some scholars that Egyptians are merely following some artistic convention and that these varieties of color do not matter is totally misleading. Usry and Keener however, are correct when they said:

> The suggestions that complexions on paintings in most periods merely reflect artistic convention, however, would be misleading. In most of the pictures, Egyptian women are dark-skinned-bright red, dark brown and so forth- just like the men. In some portrayals women are darker than men, and a woman can be darker than her husband in the picture. The exceptions suggesting a different artistic convention are mainly from sculpture from the Old Kingdom or from scenes of the dead. Various shades of pigmy on men in the same paintings indicate that Egyptian artists were quite aware of varied shades in pigment and quite capable of reproducing these realistically in their art-work; Egyptian artists had a great variety of shades at their disposal.[8]

In all periods of Egyptian Dynasties, people appear darker than their Western Asiatics in their portrayal. The complexion depictions in all period are realistic. Ancient Egyptians are like other African black people who are some time dark, light, brown and so on. Despite all these various depictions, the ancient Egyptians were black people and are Africans. These conclusions agree with the observation of an eminent scholar of Arts writing from Brooklyn Museum of Arts[9] The reason for the gradual change in color has been explained above and they apply to the Nubians themselves.[10]

The fact is that ancient writers took notice of such gradual changes and differences, but it was never on the basis of prejudice as the Eurocentric scholars maintain. Some scholars have however discussed the ambiguity of dividing people into different kind of races. Many agree that it is indeed racist and therefore, misleading.[11] Despite this ambiguity, if the world is to be divided into races, it is certain that they belong to purely African race because as Usry and Keener have said, " Africans are not homogeneous in complexion or other Physical features, any more than Europeans or Asians are. Different African peoples throughout the continent exhibit their own easily distinguishable physical features."[12] Despite all the prejudice among Eurocentric scholars, if one is asked, "To what race then, do the Ancient Egyptians belong?" Bernal has no doubt that they are Africans. He is convinced:

> that, at least for the last 7,000 years, the population of Egypt has contained African, South-West Asian, and Mediterranean types.... I believe that... the African element was stronger in the Old and Middle Kingdoms, before the Hyksos invasions, than it later became. Furthermore, I am convinced that many of the most powerful Egyptian dynasties, which were based in Upper Egypt- 1st, 11th, 12th and 18th-, were made up of pharaohs whom one can usefully call black.[13]

The physical characteristics of the self-depictions of Egyptian pharaohs and princes attested unquestionably to the fact that the ancient Egyptians were purely Africans. A close examination of the portrait of Queen Nefertiti, wife of King Akhnaton, and Thotme III who conquered the known world of that time shows the fleshly African lips.[14] African features of these Pharaohs show unmistakable blackness of these people who built the world's greatest culture and civilization. Other pharaohs with such pronounced African features are included:[15]

Despite the anti-black claims by many Eurocentric scholars, other reputable scholars have given unshakable evidences that the Ancient Egyptians were blacks. An Ancient Egyptian historian, Manetho, who was a priest under Ptolemy (300BCE) recorded that the son of Amenophis was Ramses and that the father of Ramses was a black king. Ramses the Great was considered the father of Seti who was a black King.[16]

An English writer and author of a highly reputable book, *Egypt, the Light of the World*, Gerald Massey, wrote, "The dignity is so ancient that the insignia of the pharaohs evidently belong to the time when the Egyptians wore nothing but the girdle of the Negro."[17] Sir Richard Francis Burton who was a 19th Century English Explorer, writer and linguist, discovered the sources of

River Nile in Kenya and Ethiopia. Later he wrote to Gerald Massey in 1883 saying, "You are quite right about the African Origin of the Egyptian. I have sent one hundred human skulls home to prove it."[18] George Rawlinson was quick to say that " Seti's face was thoroughly African. He has a stormy face with a depressed flat nose, thick lips and heavy chin.[19] R. T Pritchett, a scientist, wrote in his book, *Natural History of Man,* "In their complex and many of the complexions and in physical peculiarities the Egyptians were African Race."[20] In the New York Times of July 1, 1979, it was reported that the earliest Nubians did, indeed, pass on to the Egyptians the significant parts of their own culture. The digging revealed that a distinguished line of royalty, which predated the first Egyptian King by three generations, was present. Artifacts such as jewels, incense holders, and other shoe royal crowns and headdress insignia that appear precisely in Egypt a thousand years later.[21] According to Dr. F.L Griffith, from Oxford University, "More than one Nubian can be traced holding high position in Egypt or even in royal court at Memphis during the Fourth and Fifth Dynasties" of Egypt.[22]

Africanness of Egyptian People

In my former book, *Africa and the Africans in the Old Testament,*[23] I assumed that the fact that Egypt is part of Africa is well known and therefore needs no argument. But my critics and reviewers took me to task and saw that as part of the weakness of the book. I think that the discussion of whether Egypt and her ancient civilization is African or not is important and relevant in my discussion of Africa and the Africans in the New Testament.

Neither geography nor skin color, in my view, constitutes the ultimate identification, of a person, but events in history have made geography and skin color to be a very important issue. Black people all over the world, particularly in the United States of America, have been oppressed for the sole reason of the color of their skin.[24] As early as 1441-1442 Antonio Gonsalvez and NunoTristan brought ten Africans from the Sahara coast of Africa, handed them over to Pope Martin V.[25] The Pope conferred upon Portugal the possession and the sovereignty over the so called heathen land from Cape Blanco in Africa to Indian.[26] When the natives of Mexico and Peru were forced into slavery in the mines, and their death rate was too high, we learned that the honorable Bishop of Chiapa gave the slaves owners the direction of Africa in 1517 by proposing that each Spanish gentleman be allowed to import twelve African slaves.[27] The result was that about 4,000 slaves were imported from Africa every year as slaves to Cuba, Hipaniola, Jamaica and Puerto Rico.[28] Later, nearly all the nations of Europe got involved in this uncivilized and inhuman business. In the United States of America, slaves were imported from Africa and discriminated against because they were considered lower than human beings, with no soul to convert.[29] They withheld the gospel from slaves. So the issue of color and geography are quite important to those who face discrimination on the basis of their color and geography. Many African Americans and Africans faced discrimination in the midst of a White society. Many felt alienated because of the way the White people presented Christianity as a White religion. In books, movies, and photographs, Whites portrayed Biblical figures as Whites as if Blacks never participated in the events of the Bible.

One important fact is that non-Whites or dark-skinned people built the mighty empires that were respected by the White Euro-Americans. The fact is that Christianity did not begin with them and does not "belong" to them. The very homeland of Christianity (Palestine) is closer to Africa than Europe and America. The culture of Palestine is closer to Africa than Western culture. One important fact is that "Until the White European drew a political and racist map, no conscious continental boundaries existed between Israel and North Africa, and Afro Asiatic people migrated freely between what is called Africa and Asia through Ancient Palestine."[30] Egypt and Israel were closer to the rest of Africa than to the White Europeans who later appropriated their heritage. Israelites and Egyptians were darker than Europeans, and most of them would have been regarded as Black by the United States of American standard. Most ancient Egyptians were black Africans by anyone's definition.[31] The originators of Christianity were also non-Whites.

Egyptian Civilization (African Christianity)

There has been a division among scholars concerning the origin of civilization. While most Eurocentric scholars ("Pan-Babylonians") attributed this origin to the Sumerians, Africentric ones ("Pan-Egyptians") attributed this origin to Africa, namely Egypt. Orientalists generally formed two major camps concerning their earliest civilization. While "Pan-Babylonians" claim priority for Mesopotamian, the "Pan-Egyptians" make a similar claim for the Nile Valley. The contention by the Sumerologists and Assyriologists is that the Sumerians were the originator of civilization and culture and later it was introduced to the Egyptians and other part of the ancient world.[32] But most Egyptologists and Africanists on the other hand, maintained that the Egyptians were the originators of ancient civilization and culture and was later introduced to the Sumerians who eventually perfected them. There are few other scholars who believe that both Sumerians and Egyptians developed their civilization independently without any influence on one another. However, the Egyptians, Sumerians, Persians and Greek traditions attest to the fact that the ancient civilization of Egypt and Sumer originated from the Nile Valley-Africa.

The undeniable truth is that contact was maintained between the Sumerians and the Africans-Egyptian and Ethiopians. According to the inscriptions of Sargon of Agade and those of Gudea of Lagash, the main article of trade between Magan (Egypt) and Meluhha (Ethiopian) and Sumer are "gold in dust form," stones, logs, and ivory.[33] Magan and Meluhhan are mentioned as early as the period of Sargon of Agade (Third Millennium BC.). The king of Agade mentioned the boat of Magan, Meluhha and Dilmun anchored in his capital, Agade. Naram-sin said that they captured the Kings of Magan and Meluhhan where he obtained booty and gold for his temple. UrNammu also spoke about returning the Magan boats of Nanna. The economic document of Naram-Sin also mentioned trade between Sumer and Africa (Egypt and Ethiopia) during the Third Dynasty of Ur.[34]

There are similarities between the Sumerian and many scholars attest to the African religion of Egypt. The Father of Assyriology, Sir Henry Rawlinson, believes that these similarities between the Sumerians and African religion, the dark skin color of their skins, and writing, are strong evidence that the early Sumerians and their civilization originated from Africa.[35]

Professor George Rawlinson who is also a distinguished scholar and a brother of Henry Rawlinson emphasizes the uniform voice of primitive antiquity that all Ethiopians, both in Africa, Indian, and the Euphrates valley, belong to the same race.

Recent linguistic discoveries tend to show that a *Cushit* or Ethiopian race did in the earliest times extend itself along the shores of the Southern Ocean from Abyssinia to India. The whole peninsula of India was peopled by a race of this character before the influx of the Aryans. It extended from Indus along the sea coast through the modern Baluchistan and Kerman which was the proper country of the Asiatic Ethiopians; the cities on the northern shores of the Persian Gulf are shown by the brick inscriptions found among their ruins to have belonged to this race; it was dominant in Susiana and Babylonia, until overpowered in the one country by Aryan, in the other by Semitic intrusion. It can be traced both by dialect and tradition throughout the whole south coast of the Arabian Peninsula.[36]

During the course of my doctoral studies in Old Testament, we were asked to write the history of the development of Hebrew Language. I traced the origin of writing to Egypt in Africa (hieroglyphics) and my Professor argued vehemently that it was *Sumerian cuneiform instead of Egyptian hieroglyphics*. I asked him how that could be since the hieroglyphics is older than cuneiform. He responded that even though the hieroglyphic is older, it was pictorial. I consider that any written means of communication is writing. The truth is that the Egyptian civilization is older than that of Mesopotamia and the resemblance cannot be dismissed as the Euro-American scholars tend to do in their examination of these documents. In Sumer, all the gods are children of "anu," the king of the Sumerian gods. Professor Flinders Petrie was sure about this and he applies this term "Anu" or "Annu" to an original race of pre-dynastic Egypt."[37] The great British anthropologist from the University of London, Dr. W.J Perry, emphasized that the Sumerians seem to have been in touch with Africa from their earliest time and the mention of Magan and Meluhha were archaic names for Egypt and Ethiopia.[38]

The African origin of Egyptian people and civilization is incontestable. The testimonies of the Egyptians themselves are clear about their origin. The

Inscriptions of Hatshepsut mentioned several expeditions to a place called Punt. It recorded that during the reign of the queen they went as far as Cape Guardefui where plenty of gifts from the queen were presented to the governor of Punt called Pa-hehu. From the expedition, they brought back ebony, ivory, green gold, incense, myrrh and precious stones. The queen sees the Puntites as their ancestors. In other words, the Egyptians agreed that, that was their place of origin. Despite so many attempts of some of the Western scholars to identify the location of Punt in Africa, more scholars locate Punt in the area of the present Somali Land instead of Arabia. One of these scholars is Wallis Budge who believes unquestionably that Punt can be located nowhere else but in Africa.[39] He continues to support the fact that Egyptian people and civilization have African origin.[40]

Even though many modern Euro-American orientalists have knowledge of these matters, they are influenced by tradition of scholarly bias, in interpreting what Egyptians called their origin. They continue feverishly their efforts in de-Africanize Egyptian people and civilization. Moreover the Nineteenth-century scholars whose negative bias is a strong one conceive the primary prejudice against Egyptians' being black Africans. The nineteenth century Euro-Americans declares that black people are subhuman. They feverishly tried to find ways to support this declaration.

The first way of supporting their argument is to deny that ancient Egyptians were black; the second is to deny that the Ancient Egyptians had created a true civilization; the third was to make doubly sure by denying both.[41]

Cheikh Anta Diop, a black Senegalese Africanist was certain that "Egypt was a black African civilization." This civilization influenced the entire ancient Near East and all of Africa. It was the encroachment of the desert to the Sahara that made most of the Central African land uninhabitable, and that drove most Africans to the Nile Valley as early as 7000 BCE.[42] Diop continued to enumerate the reason why he believed that Egyptian Civilization is African: parallels between Egypt and other African societies, the focus of Egyptian civilization in Southern Egypt, parallel that of the kinship of Egypt with Meroitic Sudan and the similarities between Egyptian and some other African language systems.[43]

One of the finest German Egyptologist, Richard Lepsius, agreed with Professor Rawlinson when he said that the early Sumerians imported their civilization from the Nile Valley and that the Babylonian system of writings and architecture are imperfect imitation of the Egyptian form.[44]

Ustry and Keener's opinion that the Egypt of the South is different in color from the Egyptian of the North during the early period is untenable. The earliest inhabitant of Egypt, both north and South are Africans in origin. They were not Asians. Dividing them into color line is difficult to accept. The so-called black and dark color does not make much sense since all over the world; there are people of various shades of color. In West, East, and Central Africa where there were no intermarriage with the white people or Asian people, we still have people of black and dark skin colour. The truth of the matter is that there is no one who is as black charcoal in Africa. The shade of color that we call black is dark or brown in color. In both the Lower and Upper Egypt, the original inhabitants were Africans (3000-5000BCE). It was later when other nationalities came and intermarriage took place that mulattos were produced as offspring. Egypt then became " a world that did not divide continents as it is today. African and Semitic cultures mixed freely." Despite the so-called many years of the infiltration of many nationalities such as the Hyksos, Assyrians, Babylonians, Greeks, Romans, Syrians, Palestinians, and other peoples, the African character of Egypt is still evident in the shade of color of the native Egyptians. No one should deny the African character of Egypt as it is evident in the shade of the color of the native Egyptians today who would have pass being grouped into African Americans because of their color today in the United States of America.[45]

Endnotes

1. J.D Douglas Chief Editor, *The Illustrated Bible Dictionary*, Part 1(Leicester, UK: Interversity Press,1980), 419.
2. *Ancient Near Eastern Text Relating to the Old Testament. (ANET)*, 258-259.
3. Many Biblical place names occurred in the list attached to the triumphal relief subsequently sculptured by Shishak on the Temple of Amun or Karnak. in Thebes.
4. King Shabaka in 712 extradited a fugitive to Nineveh at the request of Sargon II. When Sennacherib, King of Assyrian wanted to attack Hezekiah, King of Israel, Hezekiah appealed to the Africans. The Africans defended Israel although they were defeated twice (II Kgs. 19:9; Isa. 37:9). The prophet Isaiah was vehemently against this dependent of Israel on Africa.
5. Usry and Keener, *Black Man's Religion*,64.
6. Usry and Keener, *Black Man's Religion*,64.
7. Usry and Keener, 65.
8. Bruce G. Trigger, Nubian, Negro, Black, Nilotic? in *Africa in Antiquity* 1, 27
9. Taylor, *Egypt and Nubia,* 7 See also Trigger, Nubia, Negro, Black, Nilotic?
10. Usry and Keener, *Black Man's Religion,* 67.
11. Ibid., 66.
12. Bernal, Black Athena: Fabrication of Ancient Greece, vol.1. 241-242.
13. ANET. Mark Hyman, *Blacks who died for Jesus*, (Nashville, Tenn: Winston-Derek Publishers, Inc, 1983), 80-81.
14. ANET.
15. Mark Hyman, The Blacks who Died for Jesus, 82
16. Gerald Massey, Egypt, The Light of the World, 251.
17. This was quoted by Mark Hyman, *Blacks who Died for Jesus* , 82
18. George Rawlinson, *Story of Ancient Egypt*, 252
19. R.T Pritchett, *Natural History of Man*, 124-125.
20. *New York Times*, July 1, 1979, "Ancient Nubian Artifacts Unfold Evidence of Earliest Monarchy." p.10
21. Quoted by Hyman, *Blacks who Died for Jesus*, 83
22. (Originally published by Christian University Press, San Francisco, 1998 [Reprinted by WIPF and Stock Publishers, Eugene, Oregon, 2001].
23. Glenn Usry & Craig S. Keener, *Black Man's Religion* (Downers Grove: Illinois, 1996, 61.

24. David T Adamo, *Black American Heritage* (Waco: Texian Press, 1985), 25. Reprinted by WIPF and Stock Publishers, Eugene, Oregon.
25. Ibid. 26
26. Ibid.
27. Ibid.
28. R. L Johnstone, *Religion and Society in Interaction* (Englewood Cliffs: Prentice Hall, Inc., 1975), 218.
29. Cain Hope Felder, "Cultural Ideology, Afrocentrism and Biblical Interpretation," *Black Theology: A Documentary History.* Edited by James Cone and G.S Wilmore, vol. 2(Maryknoll, N.Y: Orbis, 1993), 189.
30. Glen and Keener, Black Man's Religion, 61.
31. David T Adamo, Africa and the Africans in the Old Testament, 23.
32. James Pritchard, *Ancient Near Eastern Text Relating to the Old Testament*, 3rd Edition with Supplement (Princeton, NJ: Princeton University Press, 1969), 268-69. See also, R.R Stieglitz, " Long Distance Seafaring in Ancient Near East," *Biblical Archaeologist*, vol. 47, No 3, Sept, 1984, 1334-42.
33. Post-Sumerian documents linked specifically Magan with Egypt and Ethiopia in Africa. See Adamo, *Africa and the Africans in the Old Testament*, 46.
34. Sir Henry Rawlinson, *History of Herodotus, Book I*, translated by Professor George Rawlinson, with Essay VI in its Appendix, Book I. See also John J Jackson, *Ethiopia and the Origin of Civilization* (Baltimore: Black Classic Press, 1939), 11-13.
35. Ibid.
36. The Making of Egypt (London: Sheldon Press, 1939), 68-69. See also Africa and the Africans in the Old Testament, 26.
37. *The Growth of Civilization*, 2nd ed. (Harmonsworth: Penguin Books, 1939) 60-61. See also *Africa and The Africans*, 26-27.
38. E.A Wallis Budge, *The Egyptian Sudan* Vol. 1 (New York: AMS Press, 1976), 512-513.
39. E. A Wallis Budge, *The Egyptian Sudan*, vol .I, 513.
40. Glenn Ustry & Craig S. Keener, *Black Man's Religion* (Downers Grove, Ilinois: Intervarsity Press, 1996), 62.
41. Cheikh Anta Diop, African Origin of Egyptian Civilization, 22.
42. Diop, *African Origin of Ancient Egyptians*, 145-155 See also "Origin of the Ancient Egyptians," in *Great African Thinkers: Cheikh Anta Diop*, ed. Ivan Van Sertima. New Brunswick, NJ. *Journal of African Civilization*, 1986, 35-63. See also Usry and Keener for a good summary of these reasons, *Black Man's Religion*, 62.

43. Quoted by Ronoko Rhasidi, " African in Early Asian Civilization: A Historical Review," Ivan Van Sertima, ed. *Nile Valley Civilizations*, New Brunswick: Transaction Periodical Consortium, 1985), 15-52
44. Usury and Keener, *Black Man's Religion*, 64-65.

PART TWO

AFRICA AND AFRICANS IN THE GOSPELS

CHAPTER V

AFRICA AND AFRICANS IN THE GOSPEL OF MATTHEW

The Term "Gospels"

Matthew and Luke did not begin their Gospel like Mark, but he reported that Jesus' proclamation of the Gospel of the Kingdom (4:23; 9:35; 24:14) was at hand. Luke uses the form *euaggelizein* ("to proclaim the good news" in describing his activity (Lk.8: 1; 16:16). John does not use any form of the word *euaggelion*. But I John uses the related term *aggelia* (message) that I consider as one of the Johannine terminologies for the Gospel or good news.

During the New Testament time, the word "Gospel" did not originally refer to the books of the Bible, but it is a Greek word, *euaggelion* meaning, "a good announcement." This is the word that was translated "Gospel" in the Bible. It means a proclamation or message. It was originally used for the news of victory in a battle or the news of an emperor's birth and presence, which constituted good news to the people of the Roman world. From this, it came to mean the proclamation of the birth, life, suffering, death, and resurrection of Jesus. Late in the first century CE, the term was used to refer to the written account of the life of Jesus.

For example, Mark 1:1 opens his narrative with the word: "The beginning of the Gospel of Jesus Christ." This referred to the good news of what God had done, that was once proclaimed in ancient Israel, and now, to be proclaimed in Jesus Christ to all nations. This is the kingdom and the rule of God present in Jesus in his birth, his forgiveness of sin, healing of the sick, feeding the hungry, raising the dead, and calming the storm. This proclamation was in his teaching of parables and his entire life. Jesus was a king who was born in Bethlehem for the deliverance of people who come to him in faith. This means that the Gospel was preached orally and quotations were from the Old Testament scriptures only since no New Testament Scripture had been committed to writing.

In the gospels, we have many passages in the New Testament where Africa and Africans were mentioned. In Matthew 2:1-12, we have the record of the African wise men ("Magi") that brought gifts for the little baby, Jesus. In Matthew 2:13-19, Africa became a place of refuge for the infant Jesus and his earthly parents. Matthew 12:42 and Luke 11:31 mentioned the African Queen (Queen of the South), generally referring to the Queen of Sheba who was known for her wisdom. Matthew 27:32, Mark 15:21, Luke 23:26 recorded the story of one compassionate African man called Simon of Cyrene and his family who helped Jesus carry the cross. The city of Cyrene was in the area where Libya is today and was originally populated by black people in history before the advent and the domination of the European people.

The African Wise men with their Generous Gifts (Matthew 2:1-12)

In the second chapter of the Gospel of Matthew, we read about the visit of the wise men from the east for the purpose of worshipping the infant Christ. We were told that they followed the star with their precious gifts of gold, frankincense, and myrrh. They came to Jerusalem to ask about the place where a new king was born. When King Herod and his people in Jerusalem heard about this they were disturbed to learn about a newborn king. King Herod reacted and allowed his jealousy to overtake him. He called the "Magi" secretly to find out information about the birth of Jesus, the supposed new king. He sent the "Magi" to go to Bethlehem to find out where exactly He was. He ordered them to come back to report to him. But an angel of the Lord appeared to the "Magi" and warned them not to return to King Herod. They took another route to their various countries instead of going back to Herod.

The word *"Magi"* is a transliteration of the Greek maggoi which can be translated "wise men," "astrologers," "Magicians," or "sorcerers."[1] I believe that the correct translation should be "wise men."

The number of the "Magi" who came to pay homage has also become a subject of controversy from time to time in history. Some numbered them to be twelve, eight, and more. It was after the Gospels were written that the number three was mentioned in Christian literature. Jerome was given the credit of mentioning number three as a symbol of the "three sons of Noah."[2] To Jerome, this was the symbolism that showed that the three known continents of that time joined in worshipping Jesus.

The Bishop of Besiers, Sedatus in 589 C.E. was the first person to suggest that one of the wise men was a black Ethiopian. About this time too, the

Venerable Bede gave names to these wise men as Kasper, Melchior, and Balthasar. In the Basilica of St. Apollinare Nuovo, in Ravenna, Italy, there was a mosaic, which depicted the veneration of the "Magi" and in the mosaic Melchior was painted as having Negroid features.³ The Old Testament has been used to support the idea that these wise men were black men from Africa. Psalm 72:10-11 was interpreted as a messianic passage talking about the promised messiah. It says, "The Kings of Tarshish and of the isles shall bring presents: the kings of Sheba and Seba shall offer gifts. Yea, all kings shall fall down before him: all nations shall serve him." The passage of Isaiah was also used, "Thus said the Lord, The labour of Egypt, and merchandise of Ethiopia and of the Sabeans, men of Stature, shall come over unto thee, and they shall be thine . . . they shall make supplication unto thee, saying, Surely God is in thee" (Isaiah 45:14). Isaiah 60:6 is also used, "The multitude of camels shall cover thee, the dromedares of Media and Ephah; all they from Sheba shall come: they shall show forth the praises of the Lord." From the messianic interpretation of these passages, the tradition grew that one of these "Magi" or all of them were from Africa.

This word has been associated with the priestly class of a Persian expert in the occult such as astrology and the interpretation of dreams by the majority of western scholars. These Magis were held in great reverence and no transaction of importance was undertaken without their advice. We were also told that the religion of Zoroaster reorganized them and ordained a discipline that was simple and severe. This group believed in a messiah, in the resurrection from death and future life. But a closer look at the wise men and priests in Africa showed that they performed the same functions. In traditional Africa, no important decision is made without consultation with the priest who is also considered the custodian of wisdom. A closer look at their gifts shows that they belonged to Africa. In other words, they were African wise men who came to worship the infant Jesus. These wise men represented pagan Gentiles, who did not have the Torah, but had seen the revelation of God through stars about the newborn king. They have come to pay homage to him according to this revelation. God has never left Himself without a witness (Romans). It is not unusual for Yahweh to speak to pagan people and use them for His glory. Such instances are in abundance in the Old Testament. For instance, God spoke to Pharaoh in a dream to release Sarah, Abraham's wife. God used Cyrus, the Great, to deliver the children of Israel from exile.

Although the names of the "Magi" were not mentioned, the meaning of the descriptive name, "Magi," says something about their place of origin in Africa. As said before, I believe that the correct translation should be "wise men" instead of "sorcerers," "astrologers," or "Magicians." That describes them as the professional wise men or men full of wisdom. In antiquity, Africans or Ethiopians were full of wisdom according to Diodorus Sicilus (59-30 B.C.E.), the Greek-born writer. Although he says that some Ethiopians were primitive,[18] he was not blind to the achievement of the Ethiopians. According to him the Ethiopians were people of great wisdom and religious zeal.

In I Kings 10:1-13, one of the major purposes of the visit of the Queen of Sheba who came from Africa, was to validate Solomon's wisdom. She went to verify and test Solomon's wisdom when she heard of his wisdom. Such will make sense only if Africans were regarded as the wise people as Bailey has maintained.

When we consider the purpose of the visit of the wise men that travelled from a remote far away place we shall understand that they came from Africa. The purpose of their visit was to worship and pay homage to the newborn king. In ancient time, only the most religious class of people could travel so far for religious purpose. The Africans fit into these classes of people according to the Greek description of the religiosity of the Ethiopians. According to Diodorus[4] they are not only wise but they have religious zeal. They were the first of all men; they were pioneers in the worship of God; they originated many Egyptian customs; they were the people who sent the Egyptians out as colonists; they originated the Egyptian burial practices, the role of priests, the shape of statues and their forms of writing. According to him, the stories about Osiris of Egypt and Dionysus of the Greeks were nothing but the "glorified editions of events and exploits which were originally performed by the prince who belong to the old royal family of inner Ethiopia. Strabo, like Diodorus, mentioned the power of the priests to punish even the king of the country. He also mentioned one king who abolished this type of power accorded to the priests in Ethiopia. In their religion, says Strabo,[5] the Ethiopians honored one being as God who is regarded as immortal and caused the existence of all things.[6] The Homeric testimony, says that the land of Ethiopia is at the remotest border of the world beside the steam of the ocean. It was the place where the "blameless race of men called Ethiopians and made sacrifices pleasing to the gods, including Zeus"[7].

If one considers the nature of the gifts that were given to Jesus, they clearly fit African products. One of the gifts is gold. In antiquity African has been considered to be the greatest source of gold. In Ethiopia, it was described that gold was so plentiful in ancient times, to the extent that they bound their prisoners with gold chains. According to I Kings 10:1-13, the Queen of Sheba from Africa gave to King Solomon, the following gifts: gold, spices, and precious stones and others. Daniel 11:43 mentioned that the treasures of Egypt, Ethiopia, and Libya were gold, silver, and precious things. From the ancient description of Africa, I have no doubt that these wise men, called "Magi" were Africans and came from nowhere else but Africa.

To me the homage paid by the "Magi" may bring to memory Psalm 72:10, Isaiah 60:6, the Queen of Sheba and her visit to Solomon in I King 10:1-13.[8] Herod took the report of the wise men very seriously. That tells the importance of astrologers' prediction at that period. The report angered Herod, the king of the Jews. His wicked behaviour is indeed a reflection of our human nature characterized by selfishness, jealousy, and intolerance. Herod could not swallow the idea that the deliverance of the Jews was on the way. While the Jews and their ruler rejected Jesus, Gentiles accepted his leadership as the Messiah. Wise men from Africa were prepared to worship him whole-heartedly. They were the first people to announce his messiahship:

> And when they were come into the house, they saw the young child with Mary his mother, and fell down, and worshipped him: and when they had opened their treasures, they presented unto him gifts; gold, and frankincense, and myrrh (Matt. 2:11).

Africa as A Place of Refuge for Jesus, the Savior (Matt. 2:13-19).

After Jesus was born an angel appeared to Joseph in a dream instructing him to take the mother and the child to Egypt for safety in order to escape Herod's persecution. In obedience Joseph, Mary, and the infant Jesus went to Egypt and remained there until the death of Herod. When Herod had discovered that the "Magi" deceived him, he ordered that all the male children in Bethlehem and its vicinity be murdered. All the male children in Bethlehem were killed. After the death of Herod, an angel appeared again to Joseph instructing him to take the family back to the land of Israel. They lived in Nazareth in the district of Galilee instead of returning to Judea.

The story of Jesus in Exile in Africa, taken literally raises some questions from human perspective. The question is that of historicity and ethic. Could such thing as the slaughter of the male children in Bethlehem happen? If God actually works such miracle and uses angel to warn people to escape death, is it right to warn only one family and let the rest of the family in Bethlehem be slaughtered? The questions apply to other miracle stories in the Gospels where Jesus healed only one person at a time, and left the rest to suffer. Although the Bible is silent, one may speculate that more of such horrible stories have happened in secular history, such as the Crusades, the Holocaust, the ethnic cleansing in Kazoo, the Tutsi in Uganda, and others. The question whether such actually happened does not make sense because God has allowed that in history. The question whether an angel warned only one family and left the other is possible. The Bible is silent as to whether the angel also warned other families in Nazareth, but they did not obey. It is quite possible. In a confessional language, the author of Matthew was more concerned with the truth of the story. That truth is the divine intervention in a normal course of events and how God worked to save the infant Jesus so as to be able to fulfill the Scripture. God was already acting in the infant Jesus in his birth and preservation for the fulfillment of his messiahship.

Our major concern though is how God has used Africa and Africans for the preservation of the life of the Messiah so that He could fulfill His mission. This will be discussed further below.

The infant narrative of Matthew is made up of genealogy (1:1-17), the annunciation to Joseph (1:18-25), Herod and the "Magi" (2:1-12), the flight of Joseph into Egypt (1:13-15), Herod and the killing of the infants of Bethlehem

(2:16-18), and the return of Joseph from Egypt (2:19-23). Three of these episodes, which are dream narratives, can be described as scenic narration. The other two, which are the Herod stories can be described as straight narratives.[9] These narratives fall into two major parts corresponding into two chapters. Chapter one which did not give any indication of where or when the action takes place serves as a prologue to the narrative proper introducing us to the situation and the persons involved in it. This first chapter resolves to tell about the messianic identity of Jesus by demonstrating how the Son of God born by the virgin can also be the son of David because he is the adopted son of David and of Joseph. The second chapter of Matthew resolves to tell us about the lowly history of Jesus, showing how the persecuted and exiled child is revealed as the Messiah because His flight and exile is a recapitulation of the history of His people.[10] Chapter two is also a narrative not of places but of journeys. These journeys are the Magi's journey from the East to Jerusalem and on to Bethlehem in order to pay homage to the infant Jesus (2:1-12); Herod's soldiers journey to Bethlehem in order to kill Jesus (2:16-18); Joseph flees to Egypt for safety (2:13-15); the family returns to Nazareth when there was no more danger (2:19-21).

The fact is that the heart of the narrative is in chapter two which is the flight of Jesus into Egypt and his return to the land of Israel in Matthew 2:13-15 and 19-21. The dream narratives in chapter one and two are given neither to encourage nor to console the dreamer, nor to foretell any coming greatness, nor a revelation of secrets of the future, nor a reassurance of what is to come, but to "provide guidance and motive power for salvation history."[11] They are given as divine directives, which actually demand an action, which will set a chain of saving events in motion. In a way, the dreams in Matthew and Genesis 31:10-13, 24; 46:2-4, are unique in their forms and purpose.

The forms in which they appear link the stories of the flight into and the return of Jesus from Egypt to the Old Testament story of the Exodus. These dreams finds their closest parallel in the dream of Jacob (Gen.46: 2-4) when the patriarch was ordered to go down to Egypt which set into motion a series of events that led to his discordance being delivered from Exodus as a great nation.

The quotation formula in the narrative of the flight into Egypt (2:15) explicitly alludes to the Exodus by quoting Hosea 11:1. What it does is that it identifies the sojourn of Jesus in Egypt as the fulfillment of the Exodus experience of his people and Jesus as the embodiment of obedient and faithful Israel (Ex. 4:22-23).[12] The author of Matthew follows the Jewish tradition of reaching back to the Old Testament itself. For example, Deutro-Isaiah describes the restoration of the Babylonian exile as a new exodus (Isa. 51:9-11; 52:11-12). Jeremiah also explicitly associated the return from Babylon with the Exodus from Egypt (Jer.16: 14-15). Ezekiel also justifies the judgment to come upon the inhabitant of Judea by retelling of their Exodus centered confessional history, as a history of God's favor resisted by continuing disobedience (Ezek 20:1-26). Hosea also interprets the exile of the Northern Kingdom into Assyria as a return to Egypt (Hos. 9:3; 11:5; 11:11). The memories of Exodus and the Exile fill the consciousness of the post-exilic Israel.

The author of Matthew was certainly conscious of this tradition because the expression appears thrice in the genealogy with which the gospel begins (1:11,12,17) as a significant turning point in the salvation history, which Jesus fulfills. Matthew chapter one focuses on the Davidic Kingship and the Babylonian exile, but chapter two focuses primarily on Exodus.

In the Bible Egypt (*Aiguptoz*) is both a place of refuge in the time of distress or danger (I Kgs 11:40) and a place of bondage (Ex. 13:3, 14; 20:2; Deut. 5:6; 6:12; 7:8; 8:14; Jude 6:8; Jer. 34:1 and Mic. 6:4). The author of Matthew is aware of this fact. To really catch this depth perspective in the Matthew's story of Jesus' flight to Egypt, we need to listen to the echoes of the Old Testament. Some of these echoes are given by the place names in the Matthew's story of Joseph's flight to Egypt. The names of the places mentioned in the story are not merely indications of places but always carry a symbolic meaning because they refer to significant places in the history of Israel. In the story, Joseph was ordered to flee to Egypt. After the death of King Herod he was also ordered to return to the land of Israel as the exiled returned from captivity in Babylon. Egypt, Israel, and Babylon define the narrative space of Matthew's story and fill it with ghosts of the past.[13] These places also "determine the confessional history of Israel." Our main concern however is that of Egypt.[14]
For readers to fully understand and appreciate this passage it is important to understand the place of Africa as a place of refuge during the pre-biblical and biblical history.

As early as 3000 years, the Mesopotamians referred to Africa and Africans as Magans and Meluhhans. They came to Africa for refuge and for trade in gold.[15] Right from the time of Abraham, Africa has been a place of refuge. Genesis 12 recorded the fact that when there was famine in the land, Abraham and his family went to Africa for safety. They went there so that they may not starve to death (Gen. 12:10). However, when they got to Egypt he told a lie to Pharaoh, king of Egypt, that his wife was his sister. Of course, he planned this lie with his wife because he feared for his life. He thought that since his wife was so beautiful, Pharaoh might be interested in taking her and kill him for that reason. God, however, protected him and his wife. God plagued Pharaoh and his house and revealed to him that he had done an abominable deed by taking Abraham's wife. Pharaoh eventually released them to leave the land of Egypt.

Another important instance in which Africa became a haven of safety to the Hebrews was the time of Joseph and Jacob. God made it possible for Joseph to be sold to Egypt so that he could eventually deliver his own people (43:1). Joseph's brothers sold him away because of their jealousy. He eventually ended up in the house of Pharaoh where he prospered. Pharaoh had a dream which no one could interpret, except Joseph. Joseph was put in charge of the affairs of Egypt. He was given an Egyptian wife, Asenath, the daughter of Portipharah, the very priest of On for marriage (Gen.41: 45). God was with Joseph to the extent that he became the governor in charge of the affairs of Egypt. When there was great famine in the land, Jacob and his family, about seventy of them, went to Egypt at the demand of his son Joseph so that they could survive. In Genesis 46:2-4, Yahweh assured Jacob that He would be with him in Egypt and that He would make him a great nation. Jacob's family who came to Egypt was seventy souls (Gen.46: 47). The Hebrews went to Africa and settled in Goshen (43:11-12) for 430 years before leaving for Canaan when the Pharaoh that did not know Joseph came to the throne. If not for the refuge in Egypt, the Hebrews perhaps would not have survived.

In Exodus 8:6, we read that Aaron stretched his hand over the waters of the Nile to bring forth the plague of frogs. Perhaps, Moses did not smite the waters neither with blood nor with frogs because he found safety when his mother laid him on the river Nile.[16] Targums of Onkelos and Jonathan when commenting on Exodus 8:16 say: "However, it is not possible that the ground should be struck by you, for in it there was for you safety, when you killed the Egyptian and it received him."[17]

During the 21 Dynasty of Egypt. When King David conquered Edom, Hadad, the Edomite Prince, was taken to Egypt for safety. He was eventually given a royal Egyptian wife (I Kings 11:18-22).

Jeroboam rebelled against his father, King Solomon and ran for his dear life to Africa, namely Egypt. He served for sixteen years in the Egyptian court until the death of his father (I Kgs.11: 40). While in Egypt, he married the queen's daughter, Ano, the sister of Tahpenes. He had a son called Avia from this marriage.[18] The marriage to the Egyptian's sister and the long residence in Africa was a diplomatic act. The reason is that it had a very strong influence on his life when he returned to Israel to rule the Northern Kingdom. He fashioned the political and religious, and administrative policy after the Egyptian King Shoshenq I who was the Pharaoh of Egypt. Like Shoshenq, he united the Northern Kingdom and rebuilt important cities throughout his Kingdom to unite the people. He avoided open conflict with his traditional ethnic structures, which he learnt from Africa. Jeroboam transferred his capital to Tirza toward the end of his reign as Shoshenq transferred his capital from Bubastis to Tanis. As Shoshenq restored the Temple of Amun and increased the splendor of the worship in the Temple, so also Jeroboam restored the worship of the Golden Calves throughout his kingdom. As Sheshonq appointed his brother-in-law as high priest of Amun, and made use of his relatives and close friends in the position of priesthood, Jeroboam likewise dismissed the Levitical tradition of priesthood and appointed and gave the position of priesthood to those who were loyal to him.[19]

During the destruction of the Northern Kingdom by the Assyrians, many of the Samarians fled to Africa for refuge. When Zedekiah revolted, the Babylonians destroyed the Southern Kingdom (Judah) in 587/6 BCE. Gedeliah was chosen as the governor of Jerusalem to manage the city. However, fanatical Jews assassinated him. Fearing that the Babylonians would come and take revenge, these fanatics took the Prophet Jeremiah along with them and ran to

Africa for safety. Africa became a place of safety for one of the greatest prophets of ancient Israel.

The truth is that from time immemorial, Africa has been a place of refuge for the Hebrews and other people. The author of Matthew is aware of this long history and the role of Africa and Africans as place of refuge for different kinds of people in ancient time.

However, the main theological implication of the story of the infant Jesus coming to Egypt for safety is that the author wants to draw the readers' attention to the refugee status of Jesus. This is the beginning of his humiliation and exemplary life of humility that he wants to teach us. The consciousness of being a refugee again is a reference to the Old Testament tradition. The Law codes of the Bible repeatedly draw our attention to the fact that Israelites were once refugees in Egypt. The phrase, "for you were aliens in the land of Egypt" is found four times in the Hebrew Bible in three of the major traditions: in the covenant code of Exodus 22:21; 23:9, in the Holiness Code of Leviticus 19:34, and in the Deuteronomic Code of Deuteronomy 10:19. All of these serve as the basis for forbidding the oppression of an alien in the covenant community. The Bible says, "You shall not oppress an alien; you yourselves know how it feels to be an alien, because you were aliens in the land of Egypt" (Ex.23: 9). The fact is that Israel is very conscious of its experience of bondage in Egypt.

It would certainly be understandable for the community of Matthew to see in Jesus' being a sojourner in Egypt a reliving of the exile experience of His people. Like His people, He too had been an alien in the land of Egypt.

The author of Matthew uses the prologue as a key to Matthean teaching of Christology. Jesus is revealed as not only the descendant of David, born of the city of David itself, persecuted by the King of Israel and those in power in the holy city of Jerusalem, He is the Messiah of Israel. Africa therefore, became a place of refuge for the Messiah of Israel. The annunciation by the angel that Mary was pregnant through the working of the Holy Spirit also is a proclamation that Jesus is the Son of God. The virgin birth is an evidence of His divine sonship.

The name Emmanuel given to Jesus in the prologue (1:21), "he will save his people from their sins, is the affirmation of the presence of God with His people as in Isaiah 8:8. This shows that Matthean Christology is derived from the Bible. The Emmanuel motif shows that his Christology is a narrative in character.[20] God's presence cannot be fully understood in concepts but in related experience and testimony about that experience. Matthean Christology is a Christology from above, that is, in the story of Jesus God Himself acts. It is not through a prophet or any emissary. In Matthean Christology, the earthly Jesus is linked with the exalted Christ (1:23; 28:2).

The prologue contains five biblical quotations introduced by the stereotyped formula, "This is to fulfil the words spoken through the prophet" (1:22; 2:15,17,23; 4:14). Of course there are more quotations in the rest of the Matthean Gospel. These quotations show that it was very important that the words of the prophets be fulfilled in the person of Jesus and his story as far as

Matthew is concerned.[21] It means that the story of Jesus is an age of fulfilment. The quotation formula also was to announce Matthean's pragrammatic claim to the witness of the prophets. He was well immersed in the words or prophecies of the Old Testament prophets.

The African Queen (Matt. 12:42 and Luke 11:31)

Matthew 12:38-45 belongs to one literary unit united by the phrase "evil generation." They were probably three separate stories integrated into one literary unit that was probably taken from Mark and Q. These three units that have been woven together concern the Pharisees and teachers of law who wanted some signs, the event of the prophet Jonah, and the queen of the South. Our main concern here is the reference to the queen of the South. This episode was also recorded in Luke 11:31.

The Pharisees joined the priest in rejecting the message of the resurrection of Christ. Because of this rejection the message goes to the Gentiles who accepted that message. In Matthew 12:41-42, Jesus proclaims the fact that the Gentiles will rise up in the last judgment to judge the unbelieving Jewish leaders. This is again the reversal of expectations of the Jews who in the traditional picture, the righteous Israel will judge the sinful Gentiles. But now according to the message of Jesus, the repentant Gentiles will condemn the unbelieving Jews. This is God's concern for the Gentiles at its peak as the events of Nineveh and Jonah, the event of the visit of the Queen of Sheba to King Solomon, are mentioned to illustrate this.

In pursuance of the Matthean policy of constant references to the Old Testament, he brings to his readers the memory of the Queen of Sheba. The reference to the queen of the South is to the story in I King 10:1-13, who visited Solomon to verify his wisdom. Again according to the Old Testament, the Queen of Sheba heard of King Solomon's wisdom and went to test that wisdom. I have argued that the Queen of Sheba referred to the African queen who was regarded as full of wisdom. Some scholars have argued that the Queen of Sheba did not come from Africa. In order to refresh our memory I would discuss further my earlier understanding of the Queen of Sheba, of whom I gave fuller detail in my book, *Africa and the Africans in the Old Testament*.[22]

I Kings 10:10-13 and II Chronicles 9:1-12 represent the earliest and the briefest account of the visit of the Queen of Sheba to King Solomon of Israel in the tenth century. This brevity has probably led to much variant and further elaboration in several traditions.

According to Islamic the tradition in the Qur'an (sura 27: 15-45), the queen is a worshiper of the sun god. King Solomon sent a letter through a hoopoe to the Queen. After the Queen had read the letter she consulted her nobles. A decision was made and several presents were sent to King Solomon. When these gifts were not well appreciated, the queen herself went to Israel to visit King Solomon.

Additional account was recorded in the seventh book of the Apocryphal Acts of the Apostles. It says that St. Matthew baptized the King of Ethiopia. Matthew had arrived at Naddaver, the capital of Ethiopia where King Aeglippus reigned. There were Magicians and charmed serpents there and held sway over the people. At this time the eunuch named Candacis whom Philip had baptized welcomed Matthew. He succeeded in breaking the spell of the "Magicians and serpents. He baptized the king, court, and country, and the people built a large church in thirty days. His brother Hyrtacus who killed Matthew because he had refused to sanction Hyracus' marriage to Ephigenia, the daughter of Aeglippus, later succeeded Aeglippus as the king.

According to Jewish tradition,[23] King Solomon usually summoned all the beasts, birds, reptiles and spirits to entertain him and his fellow kings from the neighboring countries. On one occasion, all the entertainers were present except a hoopoe. When asked why the hoopoe was not present, the hoopoe said that he was searching for a city which might not be subjected to the King's authority and that he had found the city of Qitor, which was full of gold and silver, and trees watered from the Garden of Eden. The Queen of Sheba was the ruler of that city. King Solomon sent a letter through the hoopoe to the Queen of Sheba summoning her to present herself before the king. The queen complied and went to the king. At the queen's arrival, she thought that the king was sitting on water. To get to the king she lifted her dress and her hairy legs were exposed. King Solomon was disappointed and remarked that her beauty was the beauty of a woman, but her hair was the hair of a man. However, the queen ignored this remark and proceeded to recite her riddles and questions.

The Talmud has only one reference to the Queen of Sheba. In this Talmud (Baba Batra 15a) Rabbi Nathan discussed the book of Job and said that Job lived in the days of Sheba and that Sheba was not a woman but a Kingdom.

In Ethiopian tradition, Tamnin who was the head of Sheba's caravans was engaged in trading with Solomon. Having been so impressed with King Solomon's wisdom he reported this to the Queen of Sheba when he reached home. The Queen decided to see this herself. King Solomon had a banquet in honor of the queen. After the banquet, the king invited the queen to spend a night with him. The Queen of Sheba agreed on the condition that she would not be taken by force. The King agreed provided the queen promise not to take anything from his house. However, in the night the queen woke up because she was thirsty for the king had overseasoned the food she ate at the banquet. She discovered that some water was beside her bed and she drank the water. Solomon then accused her of breaking her promise and did as he pleased with her. The queen went back home to Ethiopia and had a son called Menelik. When Menelik grew up, he visited his father in Israel and was well received. When Menelik returned home, king Solomon commanded that the first-born son of Israel be sent with Menelik to find an Israelite colony there. When these men left Israel they took along with them the Ark of the Covenant to Ethiopia, which became the second Zion.[24]

The Biblical accounts (I Kings 10:1-13) state that the Queen of Sheba heard of King Solomon's wisdom and decided to visit him and test his wisdom. She went to Solomon with a great quantity of gold, precious stones and spices. She gave all these to Solomon and tested Solomon's wisdom. Woods were given to King Solomon for making tyres and harps and to support the house of the "LORD". The Bible reported that before the queen went home, the King gave her all that she desired. The story is duplicated in II Chronicles 9:1-12 with some variations. While in I King 10:9, the "LORD" was delighted in Solomon and set him on the throne of Israel because He loved Israel forever, in II Chronicles 9:8, the "LORD" was delighted in Solomon and set him on the throne of the "LORD" as king for the "LORD" and would establish them forever. While in I Kings 10:7, the queen said "Your wisdom and prosperity surpass the report which I heard, in II Chronicles, 9:6, it was reported that half of "the greatness of your wisdom was not told me." While in I Kings 10:1 the narrative ended with "And King Solomon gave to the Queen of Sheba all that she desired whatever she asked besides what she was given her by the bounty of King Solomon A careful examination of the Islamic and Jewish traditions, unlike the Biblical account, clearly revealed the legendary character of the story, while the Biblical record mentioned nothing about the Queen's religion, the Islamic tradition said that the Queen was a worshiper of the sun god and that she later became a Muslim. In II Chronicle 9:12, "King Solomon gave to the Queen of Sheba all that she desired, whatever she asked besides what she brought to the King."

Location

Another problem is the exact location of Sheba, the home of the queen who visited Solomon. Many scholars do not hesitate to locate Sheba in southern Arabia.[25] The location of Sheba in southern Arabia was given as follows:

(1) Both Assyrian and southern Arabian inscription testify to the presence of queens in Arabia as early as the eighth century BCE.[26]

(2) Domestication was widespread about two centuries before Solomon s reign.

(3) Recounting of riddles was part of the cultural conversation among the Arabians.

Of equal importance and of the greatest probability is the location of Sheba in Africa (Ethiopia). Without denying the possibility that Sheba could be located in southern Arabia, Edward Ullendorf favors the belief that it was located on the Horn of Africa.[27] Josephus, referring to Africa south of Egypt, states that the Queen of Sheba is the queen of Egypt and Ethiopia.[28] Father Mveng argues that the Queen is the queen of Saab, which, as early as the twelfth dynasty of Egypt was the capital of the Kingdom of Kush, therefore Saba should be understood as Meroe.[29] William Leo Hansberry[30] and Jacob A. Dyer maintain that the Queen was the Queen of Ethiopia, south of Egypt, but that her kingdom included the south eastern of Arabia.[31] The reasons for locating Sheba exclusively in Northern or Southern Arabia appear unconvincing when carefully examined. Although both Assyrian and Arabian inscriptions attest to the presence of queens in Arabia, none of these inscriptions mentioned any queen contemporaneous with the reign of Solomon.[32]

Hansberry and Dyer's views, that the Queen of Sheba was the Queen of Ethiopia, with her Kingdom including south-western Arabia, appear to be more reasonable in the light of the following facts:

(1) The area of Ethiopia or specifically Somaliland, as believed by this writer is noted for frankincense and myrrh trees.[33]

(2) Another closer examination of the Assyrian record seems to confirm the idea that the kingdom of the Queen of Sheba might include some part of Arabia. The Annalistic Records engraved upon slabs found in Calah written during Tiglath-Pileser III's (744 — 727) campaigns against Syria and Palestine, say that Arabia is in the country of Sheba. He says, "Samsi, the queen of Arabia who had acted against the oath (sworn) by Shamash and had. town . . . to the town I'zasi . . . Arabia in the country of Sheba.

(3) In I Kings 10:11-12[34] the reference to Ophir from which gold, precious stones and almug wood were brought to Jerusalem for the temple, is probably a reference to Africa where there was a thick forest, and which was also the source of gold in ancient times.[35] (4) The New Testament references in Matthew 12:42 and Luke 11: 31 identify the queen who visited Solomon as the Queen of the South and said that she came from the ends of the earth. The phrase "end of the earth" is usually used to refer to Africa (Ethiopia).[36]

(4) Kebra Nagast identified Candace as the "Queen of the South". (5) Although the story of the meeting of the Queen of Sheba and Solomon has enjoyed great elaboration in many parts of the world, yet nowhere is the story is "as important, vital, and as pregnant with practical significance" as in the country of Ethiopia in Africa.[37]

(5) Edward Ullendorf, an authority in Ethiopian Studies, said that it is only in Ethiopia that the legend of Solomon and the Queen of Sheba enjoy such fame and that it penetrated into the entire society and the constitution. It is considered a monument and not a literary invention.[38] He says further, "as the Old Testament to the Hebrews or the Qu'ran to the Arabs—it is the repository of Ethiopian national religious, perhaps the truest and most genuinely indigenous expression of Abyssinian Christianity. The King's throne is the throne of David and he himself is the son of David and the son of Solomon, King of Zion.[39]

Purpose of the Visit

Although many scholars place much emphasis on the trade agreement "as the main reason for the queen's visit," it appears that equal emphasis should be given to other purposes when the biblical text is carefully examined. In other words, the visit may be multipurpose. First, verses 1, 2, 4-7 seem to suggest that one of the main reasons for the visit is to test[40] Solomon's wisdom. It is noteworthy that in verse 1, 3, 4-7 the queen meant to attest the might, splendour, and Wisdom of Solomon. She came to test with "hard questions" (vs. 1); Solomon demonstrated his wisdom ("And Solomon answered all her questions: there was nothing hidden from the king which he could not explain to her" (vs. 3) by being able to answer all her questions; "she saw all the wisdom of Solomon (vs.4); the report she heard concerning the affairs and wisdom of Solomon was true" (vs. 6); and Solomon's wisdom and prosperity surpassed the report she heard (vs. 7). In this encounter it seems to me as Bailey has maintained, that the writer and the editor of the materials used the story to established and reaffirm that Solomon was the wisest in the world and even wiser than Africans whose wisdom is of high value throughout the ancient Near East.[41] Thus an African woman is used to validate Solomon's wisdom.

Second, verses 2, 10, 11-13, also seem to suggest that another main purpose of the visit was to give some gifts to King Solomon. She gave to the king talents of gold, [42] unnumbered quantity of spices and precious stones—such that never came to Solomon again (vs. 10). Such enormous gift could not be accidental, but were probably a well-planned part of her visit.

Third, there is a possibility that such great gifts may have resulted in a diplomatic trade between Solomon and the Queen, or that it may be that the gifts were given to entice Solomon to establish diplomatic trade with her.

A fourth suggested major purpose of the Queen's visit might be the establishment of a close personal relationship with the popular king. Some phrases in the text and in later traditions seem to suggest this motive. The phrase, "and she came to Solomon" (vs. 2), could be translated in various ways. It could mean entering a house in an ordinary manner. It could also mean, "to come in" implying an intimate relationship. The Hebrew verb *bo* generally means, "to come in" and is used in the Bible in several places to refer to a sexual relationship (Gen.10: 13; 19:34).

Another phrase that relates to this interpretation is "all that she desired" (vs. 13). This phrase was interpreted in the Jewish legend as an expression of the Queen's desire to have offspring by Solomon. The Ethiopian tradition in Kebra Nagast, is that the visitor had a son by Solomon. The sexual life of King Solomon, according to the Biblical account definitely supports this view. We are told that Solomon had 700 wives and 300 concubines (I Kings 11:3).

In the light of the foregoing discussion on the Queen of Sheba and the Qur'anic, the Talmudic and especially the Biblical and the archaeological confirmation of the episode and the Ethiopian traditions, the story should not be dismissed as tales for entertainment.

I believe that it is also reasonably certain in the light of the evidence cited above that the Queen lived in Africa and from there went to visit King Solomon of Israel for diplomatic trade purposes and to test his wisdom. Since according to the records of ancient Egyptians, the Assyrians, Mesopotamians and other ancient peoples, Africa was the main source of gold, timber and other precious stones for the ancient world, it is appropriate to conclude that Africa had trade interaction with ancient Israel. Therefore, the great quantity of gifts of gold, timber and all kind of precious stones that were carried to Israel by the queen as a gift for King Solomon could be samples of African products to entice Israel for trade.

Although some scholars regard I King 10:11-12 as an interpolation and therefore out of place, the inclusion of this passage appear very significant to me. It is inserted here to complete a full description of some of the abundant wares which came to Solomon that were briefly mentioned in I Kings 9:26-28 and chapter 10:10. Since Ophir is regarded as a region in Africa, south of Egypt, these passages above were meant to reveal African economic and religious contribution to ancient Israel. These products from Africa, that is, the timbers, were used to support the temple; the precious stones were used to decorate the same temple, which was one of the most important and powerful institutions in ancient Israel. This type of timber called "Sandalwood", we are told, is "bright, reddish in colour. They were heavy and closed-grained." They were also therefore admirably suitable for decorative carving" and making of musical instruments.

In Matthew 12:42 and Luke 11:31, there is a reference to the believing African judging the unbelieving Israel. It is remarkable again to come to the theme of wisdom. As discussed before, great wisdom is attributed to Africans. Those who judged during the ancient time were people of great wisdom. The mention of the Queen of Sheba as the judge is an allusion by Jesus Christ to the fact the Africans were venerated for their great wisdom.[43] This fact has been noted over and over again by the classical people and the Bible.

Endnotes

1. *Interpreters' Bible*, Vol. VIII, 140.
2. "Melchior of the Magi," Notes from *Holy Bible, Heritage Edition*, 65-68.
3. Ibid, 67.
4. Hansberry, *Africa and Africans*, 133; Strabo, 17.3
5. Strabo, 17.2-3
6. Ibid. 102,
7. Craig S. Keener, *Matthew: The IVP New Testament Commentary Series*, (Downers Grove, Illinois: Intervarsity Press, 1997), 67.
8. George M. Soares-Prabhu, "Jesus in Egypt," *Estudios Biblicos* 50 (1992), 225-249.
9. Ibid.
10. Ibid. 235.
11. bid.236.
12. Ibid. 231-32.
13. Ibid. 240.
14. See *Africa and Africans in the Old Testament*,
15. Ibid, 241.
16. J.W. Etheridge, *The Targums of Onkelos and Jonathan Ben Uzziel on the Pentateuch I-II* (New York: Ktav, 1964).
17. It is difficult to identify *these* names. However, the name Ano appeared as Anna in his Latin version and can be found in many corpuses of Egyptian names. It must be noted that there is no Egyptian sources with any name of Taphpenes as queen or princess. See Pnina Galpaz, "The Reign of Jeroboam and the Extent of Egyptian Influence," *Biblische Notizen 60* (1991), 13-19.
19. Ibid.
20 Ulrich Luz, *New Testament Theology: The Theology of the Gospel of Matthew* (Cambridge: Cambridge University Press, 1993), 32.
21. Ibid, 39.
22. Fuller detail of this discussion on the Queen of Sheba is in my article "The African Queen," *Journal of Arabic and Religious Studies*, (1990), 14-24, and my book Africa *and the Africans in the Old Testament*.
23. E.S Wallis Budge, *The Queen of Sheba and her Son Menyelek I* (London: London University Press, 1970), 37-39
24. Ibid.
25. John Bright, *A History of Israel,* 215; Montgomery locates the Sabean Kingdom in the northern Arabia. Albright, Archaeology and the Religion of Israel, 130-42,; Gus W. Van Beck, *The Land of Sheba, Solomon & Sheba*, 40-62; James Pritchard, *Solomon & Sheba*, 7-15; D. A Hubard, "Sheba" *New Bible Dictionary*, edited by J. Douglas,

Second Edition (Wheaton: Tyndale House Publishers, 1982) 1098; J. Robinson, *I & II Kings,* 126-127; D. Harvey "Queen of Sheba," *Interpreters Dictionary of the Bible* vol. 3, 11-12.
26. The Assyrian King. Tiglath-pileser IV, obtained tribute from an Arabian queen in his campaign of 732-731. BCE and listed Sheba among the tribes of northwest, Arabia. *Interpreters Dictionary of the Bible* ed. George Buttrick (Nashville; Abingdon Press, 1962) vol. 4, 311 (DB).
27. Ullendorf, "The Queen of Sheba in Ethiopian Tradition in *Solomon & Sheba,* 107, Ullendorf, *Ethiopian and the Bible,* 130ff.
28. Jewish Antiquities Book VIII, 6, 5-6. Edward Ullendorf's assessment of Josephus account is an follows: Josephus gives a slightly expanded and somewhat "smartened up version of the Old Testament story; yet the remains specifically faithful to the biblical narrative and is entirely innocent of those accretions which later on attached themselves to the queen and her meeting with Solomon". *Ethiopia and the Bible,* 135.
29. See Copher, *Nile Valley Civilization* (New Bruswick: Transaction Periodical, Consortium, 1985), 1-75.
30. Hansberry, *Africa and Africans as Seen by Classical Writers,* (Washington D.C. Howard University Press, 1977), 59.
31. *Ethiopia in the Bible,* (New York: Vantage Press,1970), 27ff
32. Beek, "Land of Sheba," *Solomon & Sheba,* 61 and 63.
33. Ibid., 47
34. *ANET.,*283
35. I Kings 10:11-12 has been variously called "editorial insertion", intrusion and misplaced text which should have been read after I Kings 9:26-28, J. Robinson, *The first Book of Kings,* 126 and 128, Long, *I Kings,* 11-20; James B. Pritchard, *Solomon and Sheba,* 10, However, these verses may be part of the story refer- ring to those whom the queen employed to bring additional gift mentioned above. See Ullendorf, *Solomon and Seba,* 107
36. (George Rawlinson identified Ophir with southern Arabia. Rawlinson, *Origin of Nations* (New York: Charles Scribers' son, 189), 2 9. Pfeiffer and Gray are not certain. Pfeiffer calls it "mysterious Ophir in south Arabia east Africa or India. *Introduction to the Old Testament,* 385. John Gray locates Ophir in south Arabia India or Africa because of the mention of apes and baboon in I Kings 10: I and II kings, 238.
37. *Biblical Archaeologist* xxxvi (1973), 42-48. According to Beck, Ophir can be identified with Egyptian "Punt" (Arabia or Somaliland). *Solomon & Sheba...* 47. Herbert "Ophir" *Theological Dictionary bf the Old Testament* locates Ophir in Somali-land in Africa where the mentioned products were attested in the ancient time. Although there is much possibility that Ophir be identified with Egyptian Punt in Africa, any absolute certainty concerning its location must await further archaeological discovery.

38. E.A. Wallis Budge, *The Queen of Sheba and Her only Son Menyelek* (1) (London: African Publication Society, reprinted in 1983), 42. After the British army defeated King Theodore of Abyssinia in 1868, the British army took to England numerous Ethiopic manuscripts and placed then in the British Museum. Among this manuscript were two copies of an ancient work highly venerated in Ethiopia? This work, *Kebra Nagast or "Glory of the Kings"* was regarded as containing an unshakeable proof that the royal house of Ethiopia descended from King Solomon and the Queen of Sheba. In 1872, King John IV of Ethiopia requested from the British government this venerated ancient document because his people would not obey him without it. Instead of sending the original copies, the trustee of the British Museum sent back one of the two copies, but kept in London the one which date 320 CE. Wallis Budge translated it into English. The phrase "gad of the earth" closely resembles the description of Kush as a remote country by the ancient Near Eastern people.
39. Ullendorf, "The Queen of Sheba in Ethiopian Tradition," *Solomon & Sheba*, 104.
40. Ibid.104-5. See article II of the revised constitution of Ethiopia, 1955, which said that "The imperial dignity shall remain perpetually attached to the line of Haile Sallassiel, descendant of King Sallassie, whose line descends without interruption from the dynasty of Menelik I, son of the Queen of Ethiopia, the Queen of Sheba, and King Solomon of Jerusalem.
41. "Beyond identification: The use of Africans in the Old Testament Poetry and Narratives," in *Stony the Road We Trod*, ed. C.H. Felder (Minneapolis Fortress Press, 1991), 181. As intellectual genius who produces at will the answer to all questions" is a reference to Solomon of later Religious Tradition
42. The 120 talents of gold amounted to approximately 2 tons, James Pritchard, *Solomon &Sheba*, 9
43. See my discussion on the Queen of Sheba in *Africa and the Africans in the Old Testament*,

CHAPTER VI

AFRICA AND AFRICANS IN THE GOSPEL ACCORDING TO MARK

Simon of Cyrene, the Compassionate African (Mark 15:21; Matt. 27:32; Luke 23:26)

Many contemporary New Testament scholars are of the opinion that information provided by the Gospels about the history of individual persons and groups is unreliable. It was generally believed that what we have in the Gospels has to do with the current and future concerns of faith. Instead of seeing the words of the Gospel as the true words of the historical Jesus, the words are considered kerygmatic in nature and focused on the deeds of the Christians whose worlds and issues are different from those of Jesus. However, there are other scholars who hold to the historical reliability of the Gospel stories.

The above opinions of scholars have some consequences on the interpretation of the story of Simon of Cyrene in Mark 15:21 and Luke. Those scholars who hold to the unreliability of the Gospel documents believe that the story of Simon of Cyrene is historically unreliable. However, those who hold to the true historical reliability of the Gospel narratives accepted the true historical reliability of the episode of the Simon of Cyrene. Without doubt, the event of Simon of Cyrene is a true historical event that actually happened. It is not in anyway a fictitious event invented by the author of Mark and Luke. The fact that the passion narratives contain some of the oldest traditions supports this view of historical reliability of the Simon story.[1] Moreover, this episode of Simon is not only one of such oldest traditions in the passion narratives; it is a case of "local knowledge" on the part of Mark regarding events surrounding Jesus' death. In other words, what we have in Mark 15:21 is an eyewitness account.[2] Each Gospel writer records the events as each sees or understands it.

Pilate released Barabbas, the murderer, to the people instead of the innocent Jesus. After the soldiers had mocked him, he was sent to be crucified on the cross of calvary. On the way to Golgotha, a certain man call Simon from the country of Cyrene was forced by the Romans to help Jesus carry the cross. According to tradition, a condemned prisoner was supposed to carry their own cross to the place of his or her execution. It was not normal for the soldiers to show mercy for the condemned prisoner by forcing another person to help him carry the cross. It appears, according to tradition, that Jesus was already carrying the cross and was dragging it on the ground because he was tired and weak. It is also likely that the executioner prefers to crucify him alive rather than have him dead on the way and therefore crucify a dead person on the cross. In such a case they drafted someone to help instead of Jesus having to carry the cross.[3] The truth is that they demanded that Jesus carry the cross on which he was to die but in such a weakened condition that he was (because of his experience the night before in the Garden of Gethsemane), he could not. He had been up all night without food and had been cruelly beaten by the soldiers. In such a weakened state, he fell beneath the heavy cross. The soldiers had to look for a substitute to carry the cross.[4] This tradition seems to be in accord with Matthew's record that says, "As they were going out, they met a man from Cyrene named Simon and they forced him to carry the cross. The Scripture says that he was coming out of the country and passing by. This latter expression has been interpreted in different ways: that he was recently coming from Cyrene or that he had been working in the fields and was just coming to the city. However, the emphasis seems to be on the fact that he was different from the bloodthirsty mob who was demanding Jesus execution. His look of shock and compassion when he saw how Jesus was treated, probably recommended him to the soldiers who commanded him to carry the cross.[5] Frans Ventur gave a graphic description of the Simon events:

> The centurion jerked his head in the direction of Jesus. "Come carry the cross," he ordered Simon. He (Simon) looked at Jesus lying in the dust, utterly exhausted. He looked defenseless, his hand limp and motionless, his narrow face reddened with blood. Simon saw how his wounds had bled into his sandals....."Where are your disciples? Why don't they carry the cross?" shouted Simon to the prisoner. Jesus looked at him, his eyes gentle but filled with pain. He looked pleadingly, as if he thirst and was begging for water, at the big man who stood menacingly over him..... Simon shuffled forward... He closed his eyes and seized it. As he stood upright, he heard the mob's derision. "There goes a new disciple!" they shouted.[6]

Sanders opinion that Simon was chosen to carry the cross of Jesus because of his color cannot be correct because Africans were held in high esteem among the Greco-Roman people. Sanders says:

> The Romans' choice of him seems less arbitrary. They choose him because of his color, which was different from theirs and which Romans had come to associate not only with race and class but also with duties that native Africans performed in the Greco-Roman world.[7]

A closer examination of how the Greek classical writers regarded Africans called, Ethiopians, makes it incorrect. Color was not an issue among the Greeks. As stated earlier in the section on Ethiopians, Africans were regarded as the wisest, most religious, strongest and blameless people on earth. The Romans also held similar ideas.[8]

This same event is recorded in the three Gospels, Matthew, Mark and Luke. The Matthean account appears to be an abbreviation of Markan's. Mark mentioned the fact that this Simon of Cyrene was the father of Alexander and Rufus who was a passerby from his country.

It is important to look at the language of Mark because the language that Mark uses to describe Simon may affect one's interpretation. Without question, the phrase "coming in from the country," and "a passerby" in Mark 15:21 suggests an alien status for Simon. Perhaps, he came to Jerusalem to celebrate the Passover or to take care of some business. He could even be a resident of Jerusalem.[9] There was a depository of Inscribed Ossuaries discovered in the grave at Kidron Valley in 1941.[10] The inscriptions mentioned the names of Simon and Alexander who were buried according to the characteristics of the Jewish burial patterns of Cyrene.

Perhaps, after performing such glorious acts of carrying the cross and preaching the gospel all over, it is possible that Simon and his family came to dwell in Jerusalem. It was also possible that he took up Jewish citizenship because it was noble and fashionable to do so during that particular period in Cyrene. The inscriptions above make it seem as if one could be right to consider Simon an African resident of Jerusalem after the event. However, at the time of the event in Mark, Matthew and Luke, he was a stranger who visited Jerusalem from Cyrene.

Cyrene was one of the African cities on the Mediterranean coast of North Africa, which was said to have been founded by the Greeks early in the seventh century BCE. About the fifth century BCE. it became one of the largest cities in Africa with mixed races of Greek, Jew, and black Africans. That there were many Africans in the city of Cyrene has been established.[11] It is known that both the Greek and the Roman colonizers intermarried with the local population very freely. This type of intermarriage also happened in Carthage, Elephantine in Upper Nile and they lived in equal terms with their neighbors.

The reference in Acts 13 to one man called Simeon, the Niger, is one of the main evidence that Simon was a black man from Africa. It should be noted that the word Niger means black. Pliny the Elder, who was one of the most important Latin writers, was the first person to mention something that related to Niger. Pliny was the first ancient writer to mention the river Niger that he calls river Nigries.[12] This river Nigries, he says, has the same characteristics as the river Nile. It produces reeds, papyrus which becomes swollen at the same time. The question of identification of the river Nigris of Pliny to the River Niger in West Africa is still debatable. However, Professor Bunbury says that in the absence of any river in the north of the great desert which fits the description of river Nigris, it must refer to the inner African river known in modern time as river Niger.[13]

Simon of Cyrene must probably have become a Christian after his experience in Golgotha. I believe that Simon, after fulfilling his orders to carry the cross, probably stood nearby to see with his own eyes what happened to Jesus. He probably asked about the background of the man who was beaten and crucified because he did not look like a criminal. As he watched him nailed on the cross, and heard him praying for His tormentors, he probably came to the conclusion that this man must truly be the son of God. That probably made Him keep in touch with the disciples of Jesus and learn more about his birth, work, suffering, death and resurrection. He, perhaps, became one of the outstanding Christians of that time. The fact that the Gospel of Mark named his sons, Rufus and Alexander, is probably to indicate that the names meant something important to the Christian community of St. Mark. It meant that these two men were some of the outstanding Christians that were known in that Christian community. Interestingly, St. Paul mentioned one Rufus in his letter to the Romans (16:13). This Rufus might be one of Simon's sons.[14] Simeon and his sons probably migrated to Antioch, one of the major Christian centers of that time. He was referred to as Simeon called Niger in Antioch. He and Lucius of Cyrene and Manaen became some of the elders of the church in Antioch who ordained Barnabas and Paul in the Christian mission to the Gentiles (more of this will be discussed later).

As already discussed, Cyrene roughly corresponds with the present Libya in North Africa. The reference to Simon of Cyrene and the name of his children shows that he was probably well known to the Gospel writers. Mark mentioning these sons of Simon might also be a way of providing some reliable witness to the crucifixion and the remarkable role that an African person has played,[15] especially since Jesus' disciples who claimed to love him had deserted him. Perhaps, the other reasons why someone was forced to help Jesus carry the cross may be a way of showing respect for Jesus since the usual way for criminals is for them to carry their own cross.

The story of Simon took up a new turn among African Christians. During the second century, Irenaeus of Lyons mentioned that the Egyptian Basilides had a totally different reading of the Simon passage. According to Irenaeus, Basilides said that it was Simon who died on the cross and not Jesus. In fact,

Jesus stood at a long distance laughing at those who thought that they had crucified him.[16] This type of interpretation continued among the Nag Hammadi of Upper Egypt.[17]

The Gospel of Mark which first recorded the episode of Simon is associated with African Christians. Egyptian Coptic Christians claimed that Mark, the author of this Gospel was the founder of their church and was the first patriarch. They maintain that the Gospel of Mark was brought to Egypt in Greek language and when the Egyptian Christians could not read Greek, he translated it to Egyptian language. If traditions are not to be dismissed outrightly, we may take seriously the Coptic traditions which also maintain that Mark established Christian missions in Egypt, Cyrenaica, and in other Libyan cities.[18]

Endnotes

1. Kieth Nickle, *The Synoptic Gospels: Conflict and Consensus* (Atlanta: John Knox Press, 1980), 40-41.
2. Vincent Taylor, *The Gospel According to St. Mark*, 587, Dibelius, *From Tradition to Gospel*, 182-183.
2. Craig S. Keener, *Matthew*, 387.
3. "Men and Women of Color in the Bible," *The Holy Bible, Heritage Edition*, (Langley Park, Maryland: International Bible Inc., 1977), 70.
4. Ibid.
5. Frans Ventur, *Man from Cyrene* (Philadelphia: Muhlenburg Press, 1962), 222-223.
6. Boykin Sanders, "In Search of a Face for Simon the Cyrene," in *The Recovery of Black Presence*, 63.
7. The issue of color is a modern ideology. The Gospel fairly followed Old Testament ideology to certain extent. See, *Africa and the Africans As Seen by the Classical Writers*, and *African and Africans in the Old Testament*.
8. Boykin Sanders, "In Search of a Face for Simon the Cyrene," in *The Recovery of Black Presence: An Interdisciplinary Exploration*, edited by Randall Bailey and Jacquelyn Grant (Nashville: Abingdon Press, 1995), 51-63.
9. N. Avigad, A "Depository of Inscribed Ossuaries in Kidron Valley," *Israel Exploration Journal*, 12/1 (1962), 1-12.
10. Ibid. 70-71.
11. Pliny, V. 8.84
12. Herodotus IV.42; See also Bunbury, *A History of Ancient Geography*, vol. 2, 74-77. Lady Lugard, the wife of the former governor of Nigeria commenting on the massive stone discovery in West Africa, suggested the possibility that the country of Chad and Nigeria were brought under the same influence of civilization which spread from Ethiopia to ancient Egypt and thence to Europe and North Africa. *A Tropical Dependency: An Outline of the Ancient History of the Western Sudan with an account of the Modern Settlement of Northern Nigeria* (New York: Barnes and Noble, 1965), 255-56.
13. Ibid.
14. Theme Perkins, *The New Interpreters' Bible* Vol. VIII (Nashville: Abingdon Press, 1995), 722.
15. Irenaeus, *Adv. Haer.* I.24:3-7.
16. A Nag Hammadi document discovered in 1945 in Upper Egypt called the Second Treatise of the Great Seth VII.2.56.

17. Aziz S Atiya, *A Jostpru Easterm Christianity* (London: Methuen and Co., Ltd. 1986), 13-48. See also his book, *The Copts and Christian Civilization* (Salt Lake City: University of Utah Press, 1979).

PART THREE

AFRICA AND AFRICANS IN THE ACTS OF THE APOSTLES AND THE EPISTLES

CHAPTER VII

AFRICA AND AFRICANS IN JERUSALEM

The book of Acts continues one of the most remarkable narratives in ancient literature. As we noticed, Luke-Acts became the longest and the most highly developed narrative of the books of the New Testament. Perhaps the books were written after the Jewish war against Rome between 66-74 CE. It is understood that the books of Luke and Acts were composed as a two-volume work each approximately the length of a papyrus scroll.[1] However, during the canonization of the New Testament, Luke was separated to join the four Gospels in order to provide the account of the life of Christ.

It is definitely certain that the unity of Luke-Act is unquestionable. They are addressed to the same person Theophilus. They both share a common language, purpose, and literary style. The same theme of the implementation of God's purpose in the world to inaugurate the " inclusive kingdom of God, embracing both Jews and Gentiles, insiders and outsiders" dominate.[2] Among the Gentiles that were included were Africans who participated in the drama of redemption.

The first part of Acts deals with Peter and his mission, centered in Jerusalem representing Jewish Christianity. After converting thousands of his fellow Jews to the new Christianity, he concludes his work by converting a Cornelius who is a Roman centurion. The second part is Chapters 13-28, which narrates a transition from a Jewish to Gentile Religion dominated by Paul and Barnabas' traveling mission to the Gentiles. Paul and his workers now see that " God has no favorites, but that every nation who is God-fearing and does what is right is acceptable to God (Acts. 10:34-35).

Acts holds a unique position in the New Testament because it contains fourteen percent of the New Testament and if added to the Gospel of Luke, it means that the author of Acts is responsible for twenty-eight percent of the New Testament. Scholars also agree that the book of Acts is the only example of historiography in the New Testament. Luke wrote the book of Acts in a historical fashion. " He wrote his history as part of the biblical history." [3] He employs in his writing of history many stylistic means such as " missionary and apologetic speeches, technical exegesis, erudite expositions, historical resumes, miracle stories, legends, dialogues, prayers, letters, we-passages, sea voyages, summaries, notes, visions, auditions, dreams." [4] From this, we can safely say that Luke, the author of the book of Acts, is the only historian among the New Testament writers. Unlike the writers of the other Gospels, from whose books we can extract historical evidence by means of deduction from the information presented, Luke presented a coherent history that, according to him, is "theologically decisive." To Luke, history has a theological purpose. The history of the early church is an integral part of the history of Israel. The history of Christianity will therefore, not be possible or complete without the Acts of the Apostles because much decisive information concerning the church will be missing.

One important observation is that there is no great zeal for mission among the Jews in Acts. To Luke, the great mission to the Jews had ended. The Church had turned to the Gentiles. No wonder it is said that the New Testament as a whole, especially Acts, is a document of Gentile Christianity when it comes to collection of the document and its canon.[5]

There are 27 books in the New Testament. Of these, 13 have Paul's name attached to them and are written in the form of letters.[6] I would like to discuss the term "Letters" and "Epistles." Some scholars make a distinction between letters and Epistles. For example, A. Deissmann in his book, *Light from the Ancient East,* maintains a strong distinction. According to him, while Epistles are materials written in the form of an artistic literary style, that generally present " moral lesson" for publication for the consumption of a general audience, Letters are non-literary materials for communication between the writers and the recipient separated by distance from one another.[7] If one goes by these criteria, all of the 21 books of the New Testament would be letters, except Hebrews and perhaps, I and II Peter, James, I John, and Jude which can be classified as Epistles.

I think this distinction may not be realistic. It is difficult to make a clear-cut distinction between Letters and Epistles because there are only few of the New Testament letters that are addressed to specific communities in specific cities but others may have in mind Christians with a particular heritage. For example, I and II John are addressed to Johannine audience. Pauline letters are to Pauline Christians, James, and Jude to Christians with a strong attachment to Judaism.[8]

The terms "Letters" and "Epistles" can be used interchangeably as far as the books of the New Testament are concerned. Pauline Letters and Epistles are meant to be read aloud. They contained the characteristics of Letters and Epistles even as far as Deissmann's criteria is concerned.

As already mentioned, it appears to me that the seven undisputed letters of Paul are the first to be written and followed by the rest of the epistles or letters. It should not be a surprise that letters were the first to be written. The reason is that the first Christians were preoccupied with the soon coming of the Lord Jesus and were not really interested in writing some permanent documents but wrote to address the current problems plaguing the churches. As a result of these, letters upon letters were written so much so that there were more letters than the Gospels in the New Testament. Twenty one of the twenty-seven books of the New Testament are Epistles or Letters. Interestingly, none of the 39 books of the canonical Old Testament scriptures were completely letters. According to the modern canonical order of the books of the New Testament in our modern Bibles, the 13 Pauline letters came immediately after the book of Acts of the Apostles. No wonder the greatest number of records of Africa and Africa are in the Acts of Apostles. While the Epistle to the Romans has only one record (Rom. 16:13), Act of Apostle has five. Acts 2:5-13, 37-41 records the activities of the African proselytes, Acts 13:1 also mentions the nameless African teachers and preachers. Acts 7:20 recorded and confirmed the African education of Moses. Acts 8:26-39 was not silent about the conversion of the African called the "Ethiopian Eunuch" and his importance. Acts 16:14-15; 40 mention the African woman convert in Asia Minor.

Among the Epistles, the book of Romans is part of the Pauline authentic and indisputable letters. In this book Paul offers the most comprehensive statement of his views on God's plan for the salvation of humanity. This letter surveys the predicament of humanity who has been alienated from God. To Paul, Jews and Gentiles are under the same bondage. He preached the Gospel of freedom from the Torah and justification by faith, and humanity's need for redemption. Among the Epistles, the book of Romans mentions one black person, Rufus, the son of Simon, called Niger who was a native of Cyrene. His father helped in carrying Jesus cross as discussed previously in the previous chapters.

The African Proselytes at the Pentecost Events (Acts. 2:5-13, 37-41).

After the ascension of Jesus, the disciples fervently remained in Jerusalem, praying and waiting for the Holy Ghost as promised them. Peter stood and preached a very powerful sermon to the people. With prayer, they cast lots and replaced Judas with Mathias. Acts 2:1-12 records the fact that Jerusalem was the center of Christianity. The entire passage under consideration is addressed to

Theophilus about the events on the day of Pentecost. On the day of Pentecost as they gathered to celebrate it with one accord, it was recorded that there was a sound of " a rushing mighty wind" which filled the entire house where they were sitting.

There suddenly appeared to the people "cloven tongues as of fire." As a result they all began to speak in other tongues because they were all filled with the Holy Ghost who gave them utterance.

People of every nation who dwelt in Jerusalem came together to find out about the noise they heard when the disciples began to speak with other tongues. With wonder, they heard these men speaking in every language of the people who were present there. That action enabled every person to hear the Gospel in his or her own language. "And they were all amazed and marveled saying one to another, Behold, are not all these which speak Galileans? And how hear we every one in our own tongue, wherein we were born?" (vs. 7-8). Those who were present include Parthian, Medes Elamites, Judeans, Cappadocians, Asians, Phrygians, Pamphylians, Romans, Jews, Creteans, Arabians, Africans (Egyptians, Cyrenians from Libya) and proselytes.

Peter again preached another sermon in defense of those accused of drunkenness because they spoke in tongue. He explained that what was happening was the fulfillment of prophecy from the Old Testament about the filling of the Holy Ghost that the Prophet Joel had prophesized. As a result of these events, the Lord added to the church daily.

My major concern in the events that took place on the day of Pentecost is the presence of Africans that is, Egyptian, and Cyreneans in Libya. It is indeed remarkable that the Eurocentric biblical scholars maintained that, since according to Philo, there were fewer than one million Jews in Alexandria by 20 CE, the Egyptians and the Libyans mentioned were not native Africans but Jews. Admittedly, there were many Jewish settlers in Alexandria, Libya, and other parts of the country like Elephantine, but this cannot be without the presence of the Egyptian and Libyan natives. The Eurocentric idea that the natives Africans could not be present on the day of Pentecost does not make sense. The policy of Alexander who encouraged his people to intermarry support that the people intermarried and they all moved freely. As there were many Jews, there were also many Greeks doing various jobs in Alexandria, Cyrene and other parts of Africa such as Elephantine. All these areas were eventually filled with mixed races. It is, therefore, unlikely that the natives were not in Jerusalem on the day of Pentecost. The mentioning of the proselytes and people from every nation shows that there were black Africans in Jerusalem on the day of Pentecost. These men were referred to as Egyptians, Cyreneans, and Libyans. Perhaps some of the people present may include Simon and his children, Rufus and Alexander (Mark 15: 21). It is likely that Simon and his son would be there on the day of Pentecost after all his experience with Jesus on the road to Golgotha and his probable conversion.

One must not be fooled to think that Africans cannot be Jews or Jews cannot be Africans. It is amazing that some scholars speak as if Africans cannot be Jews. The cases of the orthodox Jews in the modern Ethiopia called the Falashas and the Black South African Jews (Lemba tribe[9]) in South Africa come to mind. These have been proved scientifically to be original Jews, after the examination of their genes. After the authentication of the fact the Falashas was original Jews few years ago, they were airlifted to Israel. Although we were told that they were discriminated against, they live there as Jews and citizen of Israel.[10] Matthew 23:15 and Romans 2 mentioned the proselytizing zeal of the Jewish people with all their enthusiasm. They established synagogues where they and their converts met for worship, prayer and reading of the Torah in their places of settlement. Jesus referring to the Jews said, "Woe unto you scribes and Pharisees hypocrites! For ye compass sea and land to make one proselytes and when he is made, ye make him twofold more the child of hell than yourselves" (Mat. 23:15). As a result of this zeal many proselytes were converted by the first century CE. These converts were naturalized into the Jewish nations or became citizen of Israel by adopting the tenet of Judaism.[11] Those who would not accept this demand were labeled as mere "adherents," "proselytes of gate" or just fearers of God."[12] These "mere proselytes" sent their contribution to Jerusalem Temple from time to time while the other full Jews who became citizen by conversion joined the other people who visit Jerusalem for pilgrimage during various festivals. The so-called "Ethiopian Eunuch is an example of these people who go to Jerusalem annually for worship. Therefore a person called a Jew could still be African that is, Egyptian, Cyrenean or Libyan.

I certainly hold the view that Africans, especially the Egyptians, would have been the first to be converted to Christianity during the day of Pentecost since they were used to mystery religion. The idea of speaking in tongues was not strange to them (expand that mystery religion).

The truth is that Africa and Africans were not excluded in the drama of redemption. As they participated in Christ's childhood, so also did they also participate in his suffering, ascension, and in the spreading of the Gospel.

Stephen, The First African Christian Martyr, (Acts 6:8-7:54).

The Christians multiplied in Jerusalem despite the persecution that they could not be ministered to, as they should. For instance, some of the Grecian widows were neglected. When they complained, seven men who were filled with the Holy Ghost and wisdom were chosen after many prayers and laying of hands to fulfill the neglected responsibility. Among those who met this qualification and subsequently chosen were three remarkable men: Stephen, Philip, and Nicholas a proselyte of Antioch. Of all these three men, Stephen was the most active according to the record of the Scripture. He was "full of grace and power, began to work great portents and signs among the people." However, opposition arose from men of Alexandria, Cyrene and those who were in the synagogues of the Libertines. When they argued with Stephen and could not win because of power of his anointing, they became jealous, and set up false witnesses to accuse him of speaking against God and Moses. Stephen, led by the Holy Ghost, traced the history of ancient Israel and accused them of being "stiff-necked and uncircumcised in their hearts and ears." He accused them of resisting the Holy Spirit, persecuting the prophets, murdering those who proclaimed "the coming of the Righteous One," and disobedient to the law. The result of this counter accusation by Stephen was that he was stoned to death.

It might be a surprise to my readers that I mentioned Stephen as an African Martyr especially since he was not actually mentioned as coming from any of the African countries such as Egypt, Alexandria or Cyrene. Although this was not clearly stated, a close examination of the passage seems to imply that Stephen was probably from Alexandria or Cyrene in Africa. If we notice that there exists a slight flavor of Alexandria culture in his speech we shall have no problem accepting the probability that he was from Africa. It is remarkable to me that the word "wisdom" appeared four times in his speech and appeared nowhere else in the entire book of Acts. The truth is that, Africans were regarded as the wisest men on earth during the ancient time. In order words, Africa, especially Alexandria, in Egypt, was the home of ancient wisdom. This was attested to by the Father of History and Diodorus Sicilous? Almost all of the wise men and philosophers went to Egypt in Africa to learn about this African wisdom. The presence of many important African men who are prophets and teachers, pastors and evangelists support this probability that Stephen was an African. As already discussed, Simon from Cyrene who helped Jesus to carry the cross to Golgotha (Mark 15:21) became one of the prominent prophet and teacher in Antioch (Acts 13:1). Lucius was also among the prominent prophets and teachers in Antioch (Act. 13:1). Rufus who was "chosen of God" was probably the son of the Simon who helped Jesus carry his cross (Rom. 16:13). The fact that people from Africa (Alexandra and Cyrene) opposed Stephen seems to support the fact that these people might have been his own people. As the saying goes in Yoruba (Nigeria) proverbs *Ile la seni ngbe, ehinkule lota wa.* It means that most of the time our enemies are those who live with us and know us well. In biblical history, their own people killed prophets. His own people killed Christ Himself. A prophet has no honor in his hometown. His own people who opposed him stirred up other people in the synagogue and they killed him. Many scholars have claimed that Stephen is a Hellenistic Jew. This does not mean that he is not an African. We would not have any problem accepting this fact if only we remember that this period many proselytes, including Africans became Jews and even took up citizenship, new names as evidence of their complete conversion.

If Stephen had lived longer, he would have ranked with the greatest of the apostles. He probably lived for only few months if not few weeks after his election, and yet he is the ideal type of man who "being made perfect in a little while fulfills long years" (Wisd. of Sol 4:13). Within this short time that he lived, the Bible recorded that he was "full of faith and power, did great wonders and miracles among the people" (Acts 6:8). This power and faith was evident in his sermon that led him into trouble.

Stephen's powerful sermon is worth our examination. Stephen was accused of three main things (blasphemy against Moses, God and the temple). This came up after they had argued with Stephen unsuccessfully. They stirred up other people and brought up false witnesses against him. This was done out of jealousy. But one important fact is that Stephen, instead of defending himself, made use of the opportunity to preach a sermon, tracing the history of ancient Israel from the call of Abraham to the reign of Solomon and the words of the prophets.

Another important fact to take note of is the emphasis and time devoted to the part of ancient events, which took place in Africa. The rest of the period was mentioned briefly. He made references to events in Egypt about sixteen times. Egypt and Egyptians were mentioned sixteen times (Acts 7:6-40). With all these in addition to the mention of the Cyrenians, Alexandrian and the Libertines, it is highly probable that Stephen was from Africa. He concentrated on events in Africa. In his sermon, as he traced the ancient history of the Hebrews he mentioned very briefly, the call of Abraham that he used as a preliminary statement that led to the event in Africa. It is indeed remarkable that out of fifty-two verses, which contain Stephen's sermon, forty-four verses were devoted to events in Africa. It is also remarkable that more attention was given to Moses. There is an emphasis on the fact that Africa, particularly Egypt, became a place for the foundation of salvation. Moses, who was to deliver the Hebrews, was born in Africa. He was educated in African wisdom. He grew up in Pharaoh's court where he learnt all the wisdom of Egypt. Stephen in Acts 7:20-23 informed us,

> In which time Moses was born, and was exceedingly fair, and nourished up in his father's house three months. And when he was cast out Pharaoh's daughter took him up, and nourished him for her own son. And Moses was learned in all the wisdom of the Egyptians, and was mighty in words and indeed (KJV).

The Jewish historian, Josephus, confirms the authenticity of the above report saying that African prince adopted Moses and named him Thermuthis.[13] Josephus said that Moses was named by this prince from the Egyptian word, "*Mo*" meaning "water" and "uses" meaning "that saved out of it." That is, Moses in Egyptian language means, "saved out of water." In order words, the name Moses is an African name given to Moses by an Egyptian prince, Thermuthis. Josephus also reported that Moses' birth was foretold by an Egyptian sacred scribe and that this prophesies was what led to the destruction of the Hebrews' male children in Egypt. Since Moses was given special education his knowledge became superior to others because God was with him and preparing him for the great deliverance and revelation. Moses was probably educated in one of the outstanding religious centers of Egypt-Memphis, Heliopolis where philosophy, religion, medicine, law, mathematics, geometry, astronomy and all kinds of science were taught. All Egyptian priests had to attend these schools. All these disciplines mentioned above were often referred to as "the wisdom of the Egyptians." Moses probably attended all the above schools because Josephus, quoting Manetho, the most respected ancient Egyptian historian, says that Moses was one of the learned priests of Heliopolis.[14] It will not be unusual for God to use all the African wisdom, which Moses learned from Egypt, in putting down God's revelation. God does not destroy human knowledge and culture in passing out His revelation. Rather He makes use of it for His glory. Whichever aspect of African culture, religion, and cosmology that did not contradict Yahweh's revelation was used in communicating His will to the Hebrews and to the world there should be no reason why they could not be used for the communication of the Gospel in Africa. This would be true if we take note of the fact that according to Herodotus, the Egyptians were the first to maintain the doctrine that the soul of man as immortal.[15] We are also aware that Pharaoh Akhenaton was the first to propound the monotheistic concept of god, which I think was part of the teachings in Egypt. Perhaps, all these were Yahwesized by Moses. This does not mean that he copied them or stole them. But God allowed him to use the culture and the concept to communicate His revelation to the world. Stephen probably realized the importance of this and he gave some elaboration. As an African, he was delighted to emphasize the training that Moses received in Africa and that God used a well-equipped Moses to deliver His people.

The implication of the above is that African concepts are important to the development of the Old and New Testament theology. It influenced both testaments. That is why most important biblical concepts are similar to African concepts.[16]

Endnotes

1. J Beasley, C. Fant, E Joiner, D. Musser and M. Reddish, *An Introduction to the Bible* (Nashville: Abingdon Press, 1991), 389.
2. Ibid.
3. Jacob Jervell, *New Testament Theology: The Theology of the Acts of the Apostles* (Cambridge: Cambridge University Press, 1996), 116.
4. Ibid.
5. Ibid. 127.
6. Raymond Brown, *An Introduction to the New Testament*, 409.
7. 2nd Edition, (London: 1972). See full detail citation in Raymond Brown, *An Introduction to the New Testament.*
8. Raymond Brown, *An Introduction to the New Testament,* 410.
9. Magdel Le Roux, "Lost Tribes of Israel in Africa? Some Observations on Judaism Movements in Africa, with specific Reference to the Lemba in South Africa," *Religion and Theology*, vol. 6-2 (1999).
10. I have mentioned earlier that there were many Africans who became Jews and citizens of Israel during the New Testament time. Most of them changed their names to Jews name and adopted Jewish culture in their lives.
11. Robert H. Pfeiffer, *History of the New Testament Times* (London: Adam and Charles Black, nd.), 194
12. Ibid. 114.
13. Josephus, *Antiquity*, Book 2: IX.5
14. Josephus, *Against Apion I* Section 31
15. *Herodotus, Histories* II translated b George Rawlinson (New York: Tudor Publishing, 1956), 124.
16. Friday Peter Udoisang, "Africa and Africans in the New Testament," MA Dissertation, Delta State University, Abraka, Nigeria, 1998

CHAPTER VIII

AFRICA AND AFRICANS IN ANTIOCH[1]

The Conversion of the African Minister of Finance (Acts. 8:26-40)

In Acts 8:26-40 there is a reference to the so-called "Ethiopian Eunuch." From my discussion of the exact meaning of the word "Ethiopia" in the previous chapter, the translation of the Greek word *Eathiop* is misleading. Since that word does not necessarily refer to the present modern Ethiopia country but to the land occupied by the black people. Another reason is that the word Ethiopia during the classical period extended more than the modern country of Ethiopia, which the colonial masters, carved during the scramble and the partition of Africa as Ethiopia. At the same time the word "eunuch" is also mistranslated. The Greek word *eunoukos* and *saris* mean a very high officer. In most places in the Old Testament and in the LXX, it means officer rather than a castrated person. This is especially true of the man here because there is further explanation that he was a financial officer. Haechen is definitely right when he says that *eunoucox* of LXX, like both *eunoucouz* and *saris* elsewhere, frequently denotes high political or military officers; it does not necessarily indicate castration."[2] Deuteronomy 23:1 prohibits the acceptance of a castrated person into the Jewish racial or religious community. It means that if the African officer is a castrated person; he would not be allowed to worship in the synagogue in Jerusalem and to possess a scroll of the prophet Isaiah.[3] What should have been the correct translation is African official instead of Ethiopian eunuch. For this reason, I will use African officer instead of Ethiopian Eunuch whenever I am referring to this man.

The passage above concerns two main people, Philip and the unnamed African officer. In the story, the angel of the Lord spoke to Philip to go and meet one African on the road to Jerusalem and Gaza. Philip, without hesitation, arose and went. He found an African man, described as "Ethiopian eunuch," a man of great authority under Candace queen of Ethiopia. This man was in charge of the queen's treasure. He had gone to Jerusalem to worship and was coming back from Jerusalem. As he sat down in his chariot, reading the book of Isaiah the spirit commanded Philip to go and join the Ethiopian in his chariot. As he obeyed, Philip heard him reading the book of Isaiah, which says," He was led as a sheep to the slaughter, and like a lamb dumb before his sheared, so opened he not his mouth. In his humiliation his judgment was taken away; and who shall declare his generation? For his life is taken from the earth." Philip then interrupted him and asked, "Understandest thou what thou readest?" The Ethiopian answered and said, "How can I, except some man guide me?" While in his chariot, Philip explained the passage to the officer, preached to him from the Scriptures and then baptized him.

Analysis of the Passage

Acts 8-11 contains four major stories that have great concern with conversion: the Samaritans', the African officer, Paul's and Cornelius'. The fact that each of these stories made use of divine intervention and baptism is important. There is also movement in each of these stories. Acts 8:25-40 contains some repeated key words, expressive formulae and grammatical construction. "These point out the major lines of the structure and its internal articulation."[4] This narrative analyzes the line of action and the character involved in the plot. It actually revealed the presence of the narrator and the reader who are in constant communication with one another.

A careful examination of the narrative shows that the beginning (Acts 8:25-29) and the end (Acts 8: 39b-40) are chiastically arranged in relationship with one another. The spirit does begin and end the central section through his instruction to Philip, "Go up and join this carriage" (Acts 8:29, he terminates the central section by taking Philip away (Acts 8:39). Philip's question ("Do you understand what you are reading?") and the three questions of the African officer ("How can I, unless someone guides me?" About whom may I ask you, does the prophet say this, about himself or about someone else?" What is to prevent me from being baptized?) (v.36)) constitutes the central section (Acts 8:30-38) of the narrative. What appears to be the central portion of the narrative is the preaching about Jesus and the baptism of the African financial officer.

This narrative emphasizes two main things: he was an "Ethiopian" and a "eunuch." His name is not given. Instead of that he is introduced into the narrative five times without the clue whether he is a Gentile or Jew. In this narrative Luke wants to show that the Gospel is also for the peoples who dwell on the outermost fringes of the inhabited world. As an African, a high officer, and example of "not my people" who became "my people," he has come to the brightness of the light of Christianity.

Here Philip's first question introduces the officer one by one. First, the officer does not understand what he reads because he has no one to guide him. Through the instruction of the spirit, Philip comes up and sits with him in the carriage. Again the African officer does not know about whom the prophet speaks. Philip then explains the Scripture passage with the preaching of the good news. The officer wonders what prevents him from being baptized. There is nothing and Philip baptized him. As it stands, the narrative flows from a lack of understanding of the Scripture through the preaching of the gospel of Jesus and the baptism of the African officer.

Notice how receptive the African officer is to Philip (Acts 8:31). His hospitality is demonstrated in his invitation of Philip to join him and travel with him in his chariot (8.31). As they travel together and the African officer learns the truth he submits to baptism. This hospitality is based on the usual generosity of the Africans. Apart from that, the Holy Spirit was also in control of the whole affairs as evident in the generosity and the submission of the African to baptism by Philip.

Identification of the Candace

It is also important to take note of the status of the African (Ethiopian). He was "a foreign mediating broker who, aside, from being a man of means" was said to be in charge of the Candace's treasure.[5] The fact that he was able to travel so far on a sofa-driven chariot simply to worship shows that he is an important person known far and wide. His prestige is not of local one but from the distant land of Africa.[6] The powerful black man who is a minister in charge of the treasures of the Meroitic Candace, though a visitor of some distinction from a far away foreign land of Africa, has demonstrated the very symbols of great status as far as the Roman social status is concerned, mainly literacy, possession of a carriage and horses, and personal servants. I find it remarkable that of all the foreigners who were probably involved in this pilgrimage, the only person picked to report on was an African from a far away land. Perhaps, Luke picks him and singles him out as a result of the importance attached to the Africans in the Old Testament and the Greco-Roman proverbial ranking of the Africans as wealthy, wise and militarily mighty. Before we proceed, let us examine the Old Testament Scriptures and the Greco-Roman documents and their view of the African people.

Who is this Candace? Or who is the Ethiopian Eunuch? The majority of scholars have associated this Candace with the queen of Ethiopians in the Kingdom of Meroe. One fact is that many queens by the name Candace were mentioned from the classical period and other sources. One queen Candace met Alexander.[7] Strabo also mentioned other Candaces who were taken prisoners by Petronius.[8] Pliny the Elders also mentioned that the expedition sent by Nero to explore Ethiopia reported about one queen Candace. One may then ask: to which queen Candace is Acts. 8:27 referring to? There is no doubt the Ethiopian Eunuch baptized by Philip can be associated with a servant of one of the queens in Africa, but not necessarily the present country of Ethiopia or to the Queen of Sheba as believed by the present day Ethiopians. The term has been used to refer to the farthest of humankind. They live in a place where the sun sets. As discussed earlier, it literally means "burnt-faced," referring to the black people and their Diaspora, including the present nation of Ethiopia, but not limited to it.[9]

The Greco-Roman description of the African people as wealthy and powerful is also in accordance with the above biblical descriptions. The natural products of inland Africa were copper, iron, gold, and various kinds of precious stones, ebony trees, palm, and the Persea and carob trees, which were introduced to Egypt from Ethiopia.[10] Diodorus mentioned the king of Ethiopia, Sabach, who invaded Egypt, as noted for kindness and zeal more than his predecessors.[11]

Tradition has it that this Ethiopian officer became an apostle not only to the black people of Africa, but also to Arabia Felix and Taprobane (Ceylon) and that St. Matthew even came to Ethiopia to follow up the evangelization of this Ethiopian officer.[12]

What is important in all these is not only that the author of Acts singles out the black man from Africa with a clear description of his high social status, thus following the Old Testament and the Greco-Roman traditions, there is a high recognition of Africans and there is no prejudice of any kind against the African people. More importantly, the generosity and the humility demonstrated by the African officer are remarkable. Despite all the power at his discharge, he humbles himself before the deity's representative. It shows that God demands submission from people of high power in order that they may share in the truer and greater ultimate powerful order.

This story shows that the Bible had had a place in the lives of Africans ever since its existence as a body of sacred writings to the present day. Even before the Old Testament reached its final stage as the Scripture of the Christians in about 100 CE, Africans were already acquainted with it and using it according to the account of Luke that the African returning from worship in Jerusalem was reading the book of Isaiah 53. This story points to the fact that Christianity arrived in Africa prior its arrival in Europe. Perhaps, that could also accounts for the love affair of Africa and Africans with the Bible.[13]

The African Prophet and Teachers in Antioch (Acts 13:1)

The City of Antioch

The event took place in Antioch. It will therefore, be relevant to discuss what the city looked like during the biblical time. Antioch was located in the northwest of Syria, the modern city of Antakya, Turkey. It ranked with Rome and Alexandria as one of the three greatest cities of the Greco-Roman world. It was an early center of Christian expansion and named after Antioch, the father of the founder, Seleucus. Antioch was an important city in antiquity because of the fact that it was the center of trade between the Mediterranean world, the Syrian hinterland, and the Eastern countries. Its harbor in the Orontes was one of the principal harbors of the Eastern Mediterranean. Antioch was also located on the best land route to Asia Minor, Syria, and Palestine. All these contributed to its prominence and the unique role it played in early Christian mission.

From the earliest time, Antioch was occupied by traders until the time of Alexander the Great who spread Hellenism throughout the Near East. Seleucus played a great role in the establishment of the Greek and Macedonian culture. During his time the city was mixed with Greek, Macedonian and the native Syrians, and some Jewish colony that were given as a reward of their services in Seleucus army. Antioch became the capital of Seleucid dynasty in Syria. Antioch eventually became an important political and commercial city and attained great prosperity with flourished Greek civilization and with great contact with oriental cultural and religious ideas. The Romans occupied Syria in 64 BCE. Antioch then became the capital and the military headquarters of the new Syrian province. At this time the city was enlarged and beautified by the Romans, namely, Julius Caesar, Augustus, and Tiberius with the assistance of King Herod. They built new roads and expanded the ports with some security and police protection to the Christian missionaries. There was a general peace in Antioch at this time.

That enabled the Jewish colony located in Antioch to apply its ceremony and teaching many Gentiles who found the teaching of Jewish monotheism and ethics more satisfying than the beliefs of the oriental philosophies and religions. Among those attracted to Judaism was Nicolaus of Antioch who later became one of the seven deacons of Jerusalem (Acts 6:5).

When a persecution broke out in Jerusalem after the execution of Stephen, some Christians fled as far as Phoenicia, Cyprus, and Antioch preaching Jesus to the Jews only. However, when some of these Christians reached Antioch, they started preaching to the Greek-speaking Gentiles from Cyprus and Cyrene and others (Acts 11:20). Many were converted (Acts 11:21). The Jerusalem elders sent Barnabas to Antioch. When Barnabas saw that the work prospered he sent for Paul to join him in Antioch (Acts 11:24-26) and they both stayed there for a year teaching and preaching even on the street. It was in Antioch that the disciples were first called Christians, which probably means followers of Christ (Acts 11:26). A great number of people believed and were taught by Barnabas, Paul, Symeon Niger, Lucius of Cyrene and Manaen who were designated as prophets and teachers. The group of Christians in Antioch was also called ecclesia or church, which refers to the group of faithful persons in the city also called "brethren" (Acts 15:1, 32-33), and disciples (Acts 11:26 and 14:28).

The Gentiles and the Jewish Christians probably met separately but later some strange teachings crept into the church in Corinth. There was different information about Jesus going around in the church in Antioch. According to the book of Acts when a famine occurred in 46 C.E the community at Antioch sent Barnabas and Paul took some financial aid to the brethren (Acts 11:27-30). During this visit, the problem of application of the law to the newly converted people was discussed between Barnabas and Paul and the Elders in Jerusalem (Acts 15:1ff). Paul believed that the Jewish law should not be applied to the newly converted Gentiles and some of the agreement was reached (Acts 15:19-35; Gal. 2:1-10). This agreement must have been contained in the letter addressed to the Church in Antioch in Acts 15:23-29. Peter himself visited Antioch and ate with the Gentile Christians (Gal. 2:11-12). James, instead of going sent emissaries, Judas Barsabbas, and Silas to Corinth in order to persuade the Jews to understand the situation of the Gentiles. Eventually, Peter and Barnabas broke away from Paul after this argument (Gal. 2:11-13).

Endnotes

1. The topic of this chapter does not mean that the African Minister of Finance was in Antioch. He has left Jerusalem and was traveling on the road. Since no one actually knows where he was, the topic of this chapter is used for understanding.
2. Ernst Henchmen, *Acts of the Apostles A Commentary* (Philadelphia: Westminster Press, 1965), 310.
3. Ibid.
4. R.F O'Toole S.J, "Philip and the Ethiopian Eunuch" (Acts VIII 25-40," *Journal of New Testament Studies* 17 (1983), 25-34.
5. Candace in Latin form of Meroitic term, Kandake, queen mother. Abraham Smith,
6. Do You Understand What You are Reading?" A Literary Critical Reading of the Ethiopian (Kushite Episode (Acts 8:26-40), *Journal of Interdenominational Theological Center*, 22 (1994): 48-70.
7. Ibid.
8. *Peudo-Callisthenes*, III.18. See also Edward Ullendorff, "Candace (Acts VIII.27) and the Queen of Sheba" *Journal of New Testament Studies* 2 (1956), 53-56.
9. Strabo, XVII, 820. See also E. Ullendorff, 53.
10. The Old Testament (Hebrew Bible) referred to Africans as Kushites. Many passages attested to the high esteem attached to Africans. The LXX translated the word Kushites to Ethiopia. Certainly, the LXX from which the author of Acts has access repeatedly casts the Africans as wealthy. Deutro-Isaiah mentioned the wealth of Egypt and the merchandise of Ethiopia (45:14). As mentioned before, Daniel 11:43 also referred to the treasures of gold and silver, and all the precious things of Egypt and Libyans and the Ethiopian. The writer seems to assure the persecuted ones during the Maccabean period that even though the wicked seem to prosper and conquer even the powerful nations (Egypt and Africa); his (Antiochus Epiphanes') end is at hand. Thus, ancient Africa is recognized as wealthy nations throughout ancient Israel.

    The Psalter is not silent about the riches as tribute and worship brought to God in Jerusalem sanctuary (Psalm 68:29-36). Egypt will bring bronze and Kush will stretch out her hands." The solemn processions are seen, O God, the processions of my God, my King, into the sanctuary the singers in front, the minstrels last, between them maidens playing timbrels: 'Bless God in the great congregation, the LORD, O you who are of Israel's fountain.' Psalm 68:29-33 reflected Deutero-Isaiah's universalism. In the feast at Jerusalem, the cult community, after acknowledging the kingship of Yahweh over the covenant community, from the beginning to the present, the congregation expected that "in the days to come Yahweh would be King over the universe" and world empire to be established on earth. When this empire is established, all nations will be represented acknowledging Yahweh and bringing homage to him (68:31). In this case, Egypt, Pathros and Africa (the most venerable and also the most remote and exotic of the ancient nations) represent the entire world coming to Jerusalem and acknowledging Yahweh with their gifts. It is noteworthy that only two nations from Africa were mentioned to represent the entire world. It means that the Psalmist knows how wealthy and important these African nations were and that it suffice to just mention these two African nations to make the point of how far reaching (geographically) and rich (economically) will be this universal appeal of Yahwism.

The veneration of the African wisdom is explicit in the story of the visit of the Queen of Sheba in I Kings. One of the purposes of the visit was to validate Solomon's wisdom. This will only make sense if Israel considered African wisdom as exceptional.

She went to Solomon with great quantity of gold, precious stones and spices and she tested Solomon's wisdom.

The military prowess of Africans also resounds in the LXX as in 2 Sam.18: 21 ff. A careful examination of the passage shows that the idea that the Kushite is either a slave or mercenary from Africa has no basis. The Kushite (African) could not be a slave because if he was a slave, he would not be the right military man to send to the King. Normally it is not a military man of the lowest rank that is usually sent to the King. If he had been a slave or a mercenary, he would not have known the Court language so well. Ahimaaz was refused at first when he requested the permission to deliver the news of victory to the King. This is probably because he lacked the appropriate court language. He was only reluctantly allowed to go later after the African had been chosen instead to deliver the message of victory to the King.

In many passages there is the recognition of African military might. The Chronicler demonstrates that no matter how powerful an army is, including African military might, Yahweh can destroy it. In other words, Yahweh is even more powerful than African military force, which is recognized, in ancient Israel as mighty and fierce.

Isaiah 18:1, 2 refers to Africa as a nation tall and smooth and mighty in conquering. Certainly, the author of Acts was aware of this portrait of the Africans and the description of this nation as wealthy, and wise.

11. Diodorus, 3.8.5; 3.11; 3.2-3.7
12. Ibid. 120-123.
13. "Men and Women of Color in the Bible," The *Holy Bible, Heritage Edition*, 77.

14. Jonathan Draper, "Ethiopia Shall Soon Stretch out Her Hands to God," *Bulletin for Contextual Theology in Africa* vol. 6, No 1 March 1999, 4.

CHAPTER IX

AFRICA AND AFRICANS IN PHILIPI, EPHESUS, AND CORINTH

Lydia, the African Woman Convert in Philippi (Acts. 16:14-15, 40)

Paul left Troas to Samothracia, to Neapolis, and from there to Philippi. During his brief stay at Philippi, a number of things happened. First on the Sabbath day he went out to the city to a riverside where prayer was being said by women. They met a certain woman called Lydia, a seller of purple from the city of Thyatira. She was a religious woman who listened to Paul's preaching and believed and was baptized. She generously invited Paul to stay in her house for some days.

The City of Philippi

I will like to discuss briefly the city of Philippi in the ancient time and in the time of Paul. Philippi was in the east Macedonia in the region bonded by Strymon Rive on the west and the Nestos River on the east. The city was about ten miles inland from the Aegean Sea. The overland route ran through the plain and directly through the city from Asia to the West and the military and commercial way.

Diodorus reported that settlers who came from offshore Island of Thasos originally occupied the site of Philippi.[1] It was believed that Callistratus, the orator, who ran for his life from Athens in 361 BCE. was very active in making this settlement positive and naming Philippi Krenides, referring to the springs and water in the vicinity. In 356 BCE Philip II, King of Macedon was in Krenides and increased the size of the city and the inhabitants, and changed the name of the city to Philippi his own name.[2] He probably built the walls around Philippi.

In 335 BCE when Alexander the Great, in his attempt to conquer the world, marched from Amphipolis, went through Philippi. In 167 BCE when the Romans divided Macedonia into four districts, Amphipolis became the capital instead of Philippi. In 42 BCE. The famous battle of Philippi was fought and Antony and Octavian defeated Brutus. Philippi later became the Roman colony and many Roman soldiers were settled in Philippi. When Octavian was dispossessed from their home in Italy, he and his supporters went and settled in Philippi and the colony was therefore refounded with the title *Colonia Julia Philippensis* and when Octavian received from the Senate the designation Augustus, the city was renamed *Colonia Augusta Julia Philippensis* in 27 BCE.

Excavations were conducted at the ruins of Philippi by the Ecole Francaise d'Athens from 1914-1938. As revealed in the inscriptions discovered, the population of Philipi included Thracians, indigenous people who descended from the settlers brought by Callistraatus and Philip II and the Romans colonists brought by Anthony and Octavian. The religions in Philippi were composite: Thracian god *Liber Pater* and *goddess* Bendis, The Greek Athena, the Roman Jupiter, Mars, and the emperor cult, the Anatolian Cybele, and the Egyptian Isis, Serapis and Harpocrates.[3]

The name Philippi appears in Acts 16:12, 20:6, Philippians 1:1, and I Thessalonians 2:2. In Acts 16:13 Paul and his party are said to be going out "outside the gate to the riverside" in order to find a place of prayer. Where Jewish women assembled, Paul preached to them. The Jews may have been required to hold their meetings at this distance so as not to introduce a new or strange cult. Lydia was introduced as a seller of purple goods. A Latin inscription at Philippi contains the word *PVRPVRARI*. This is independent evidence that commerce in purple existed in Philippi. The two Latin crosses found there which may belong from the second to the fourth century, the Christian epitaphs, and the two large basilicas of the fifth and sixth century, support the existence of later Christianity in Philippi.[4] The church in Philippi was Paul's first congregation in Europe to which he later wrote his Epistle in the eleventh book of the New Testament canon.

Lydia of Philippi

The name, Lydia appears to bring some controversies among scholars. There is no unanimous agreement among scholars concerning this name. One scholar said that Lydia was a well-known name from the city of Thyatira (Rev. 2:18) famous for the purple dyeing industry.[5] Another said that the name Lydia is both a personal name and ethnic name, which refers to an African city in Libya, thus referring to her as an African woman of Diaspora. It appears that Thyatira where she came from was a city in the district known as Lydia in the Persian period.[6] This city was called Lud in the ancient world, especially in the Bible (2000-1550 BCE). Lydia seems to have its root from the singular word Lud and plural Ludim. Since it was not unusual for people to bare ethnic names in the ancient Near East, as said above, Lydia is therefore both a personal and ethnic name given to the woman.[7] In the period of the Old Testament (Gen. 10) Ludim was identified with the Hamites. In Jeremiah 46:9 it was associated with Ethiopia. In Ezekiel 27:10 they are associated with Put (Libya). Lud is again associated with Ethiopia in Ezekiel 30:5 and Put, was also allies of Egypt. Whichever way one sees it, the Ludites were associated with Africans. It is possible that this woman was an African Diaspora in Philippi doing her business there. The Jewish historian, Josephus considers Lud to be Lydians.[8] Wenham also maintains that they were not Semites but Hamites.[9] The truth is that the Libyans whose African origin was doubted by Eurocentric scholars whom some Eurocentric scholars were originally a black race in Africa. Their cities, like most of the North African cities such as Egypt, fell into the hands of primitive raiders, invaders, settlers and colonizers from the ancient world. Yet their Negroid characteristic is still obvious. Unfortunately most modern Libyans prefer to associate themselves with the white race due to indoctrination and perversion of ancient history. In the light of the biblical record associating Ludim with Ethiopians and the ancient record doing the same thing, it is reasonable to believe that the first convert in Europe was an African businesswoman who lived in Philippi.

Paul, in his missionary journey stopped at Philippi. Luke, the author of Acts seems to have some special interest in Philippi. He styled it the leading city of the district of Macedonians. The city of Philippi had a prestige of its own.

Of all these women, Lydia's name was the only one mentioned. She was a successful businesswoman. She was deeply religious. Although she was a well-to-do woman, she was not ashamed to associate herself with an unimportant prayer group by the river. Thyatira was a Lydian city famous for trade in purple dyes.[10] It is further suggested that if the Lydian is correct, her name may be Euodia or Syntyche, the names mentioned in Philippians 4:2. Lydia was not a Jew by birth. She probably grew up as an unbeliever. Paul preached to her and she became a believer and was baptized, including her household. In fact, she could not tolerate seeing Paul and his friends staying elsewhere. Her faith was linked with action.

Despite Paul's brief stay in Philippi, he was able to establish the church and put her on a good footing. He had a great and peculiar affection for this church because of the church's unwavering loyalty to her founder (Phil. 1:3-5). From Luke's account, it was customary for Jews to gather by the river at Philippi for prayer. These women were Paul's first congregation in the city of Philippi. It is very interesting and remarkable that this congregation consisted of women and no man, no building, no prestige or influence in the city. Yet the church grew into one of the strongest, most generous, and less troublesome churches founded by Paul.

Paul received some gifts, and financial aid from the church at Philippi alone (Phil. 4:10). No other epistle is filled with the expression of joy like that of the Epistle to the Philippians. The Jews never troubled Paul during his brief stay at Philippi. The only trouble he had there was from the heathens. This must be as s result of the fewness of the Jews in Philippi and the pervasive influence of the powerful and committed African woman called Lydia.

Like most Africans, the most notable thing about Lydia is her hospitality. As soon as she was baptized she invited Paul and his friends to her house. It was very unusual because some women would have hesitated to invite a Jewish rabbi and his friends to her house more so when this type of rabbi was a radical one. However, she fearlessly insisted that they must come to her house despite the embarrassment that the strangers might cause, and they did. She displays a human grace by sharing her home with other people. To do that is to share one's life because by doing that she was offering them "an entrance into the sacred precincts" of her life. In Christianity, to display hospitality is to express in action that grace for which Christ died and rose again from the dead. It is a demonstration of Christian brotherhood and family of God. Jesus makes it one of the requirements of life in his kingdom. "For I was a hungered, and ye gave me meat: I was thirsty and ye gave me drink: I was a stranger, and ye took me in" (Matt. 25:35). Hence, the otherwise unknown African, called Lydia, rose to the position of dignity and honor when she gave her house to the apostle Paul and his company to stay in. Again this has been the virtue of most African people even though they have been robbed and taken advantage of by foreigners and colonial powers. Missionaries who have been to the African continent will attest to the exceptional generosity of the African people.

The African Missionary and Teacher in Ephesus and Corinth, Apollos of Alexandria (Acts 18:24-28; 19:1)

Before discussing the above passages, which involve an African teacher and orator, it will be appropriate to discuss the cities where these events took place, that is, Ephesus and Corinth in antiquity.

The event mentioned above took place in Ephesus, which was a large seaport city in the Roman province of Asia. It was a commercial and religious center where Paul worked for a long period of time. Acts 19:8, 10 said that he taught in the synagogue for three months and after that he was in the hall of Tyrannus for two years. Acts 20:31 gives a round figure by saying that Paul was there for three years. The name Ephesus appears in the book of Ephesisans 18:27. The Ephesians is also referred to in Acts 19:28, 34, and 35. Trophimus, the Ephesians was spoken of in Acts 21:29. Ephesus is also mentioned in I Corinthians 15:32; 16:8; I Timothy 1:3; II Timothy 1:18; 4:12; and Revelation 1:11; 2:1.

Ephesus

Ephesus was the most favorable city in the west coast of Asia Minor because "it emptied into a good harbor and also gave excellent access to the valleys of both the Hermus and the Maeander." The first inhabitant of Ephesus, according to Strabo, were the Carians and Leleges who were eventually driven out by androclus, the son of the King of Athens who led the Ionian colonization.[11] He was later regarded as the founder of Ephesus. In Ephesus, there existed from the beginning the cult goddess called Artemis. The first temple of Artemis was built by Cherisphron who was an architect. Croesus, who came to the throne of Lydia in 560 BCE, boasted of his conquest of virtually all the nations of west Halys River. The first city he attacked was Ephesus.[12] At the heat of Croesus' siege, the Ephesians dedicated their city to the goddess of Artemis by attaching rope from the temple to the city wall.[13] In about 546 when the Persian King Cyrus defeated Croesus, General Harpagus systematically overcame the Ionian cities, including Ephesus.

It was reported, according to tradition, that the very day that Alexander was born; a certain Herostratus burned the temple of Artemis in Ephesus.[14]

In 334 BCE Alexander the Great conquered the Persians and immediately Ephesus came under the Macedonian rule. The citizen of Ephesus set to rebuild the city and Alexander promised to pay for the cost, provided they give him credit for it. Unfortunately, the citizen refused and flattered him that it was inappropriate for a god to dedicate offering to gods.[15] Lysimachus, the successor of Alexander was considered the builder of modern city of Ephesus by bringing to Ephesus people from Lebedos and Colophon. He rebuilt the city on a higher ground and requested that the citizen move to the new place. When they refused, he blocked the sewers, during a heavy rain. When the old city began to stink, he asked them whether they were ready to move to the new location. The citizens were glad to have a new place to move to. Lysimachus was happy to see them moving. He gave the city a new name, *Arsinoe*, in honor of his wife's name.

Ephesus came under Seleucid King Antiochus I after Lysimachus was defeated by Seleucus I. In 190 BCE, the Romans defeated Seleucid King Antiochus III at the battle of Magnesia and Ephesus later became a Roman city.

The victory of Pompey and the death of Mithradates brought the whole of east Mediterranean under the Roman rule by 64 BCE. Under the reign of Caesar Augustus Ephesus enjoyed the general existing peace. At this time the Ephesians dedicated a sacred precinct to Rome and Caesar. This made them achieve the chief place and great glory in Asia.

Many archaeological excavations were conducted in the city of Ephesus as early as 1863. The wall of the temple of Artemis was found in May 1869 by J.T. Wood. Another remains of another temple, which probably was built during the time of Alexander, was also uncovered. This was the temple described as one of the seven wonders of the ancient world which the adherents feared might come to nothing through the preaching of Paul in Acts 19:27. It diminished at the coming of Christianity and was finally burned by the Goths in C.E 262. Other buildings were found not far from the agora, the library and a temple, which was probably dedicated to the African god Serapis. Other temples found included the temple erected by the Ephesians for the worship of the emperor.

Christian tradition connects John the Apostle and evangelist with Ephesus. In fact, the name Ayasoluk, which was attached to the village and also to the hill in the vicinity of the Artemission, derived from the Greek word Agios *Theologos* that literally means "The Holy Theologians," was the title given to John in the Eastern Church. From this hill, John viewed the idolatrous worship of the Artemision. Tradition says that he was also buried on this same hill. A church was also built on this tomb called the Church of Saint John, the Theologian in Ephesus. Finding shows that between the stadium and the harbor, a large church was also built on its foundation of a pagan building. It appears to have consisted of two churches arranged one behind the other and was called a double church. An inscription found there showed that it was a church referred to as the famous Church of the Virgin Mary, in which the Council of Ephesus met in 431 C.E.[16] On the North East of the slope of the Panajir Dagh, is located a Catacomb of the Seven Sleepers. The legend says that during the persecution of the Decius (250 C.E), "seven young men were sealed in a cave, fell asleep, and only awoke under Theodosius II (407-450) to testify again to their Christian faith. Upon their death they were buried in a cave and a church was built over their cave and the graves of many other saints were put in the same area.[17]

An inscription was found in the ruins of a gateway near the agora, which also bear witness to the victory of Christianity in Ephesus. This inscription was on a rectangular stone, which had evidently served as the base for an idol of Artemis, and on which a Christian had put up a cross. Referring to the Cross, the inscriptions say: 'Demeas has removed the deceitful image of the demon Artemis and in its place put this sign which drives away the idols, to the praise of God and of the cross, the victorious, imperishable symbol of Christ'.[18]

Corinth

Corinth was mentioned in Acts 18:1, 19:1; I Corinthian 1:2; II Corinthian 1:1; II Timothy 4:20. We may need to narrate the event that led to the appearance of Corinth in the above passages. Corinth was the capital of the Roman province of Achaia. Strabo gave the description of Corinth after it was restored by the Romans in 44 BCE. An excavation was conducted by the American school of Classical Studies in Athens in 1896. It was discovered that by the eight century BCE Corinth had found colonies at Corfu and Syracuse. In the seventh century Cypselus was a tyrant at Corinth and his son succeeded him under whom Corinth reached the height of her power and prosperity. The city was famous for bronze work, and its products were carried far and wide by extensive shipping. After Corinth survived the Peloponnesian and Corinthian Wars, it came into conflict with Rome and was eventually sacked, captured, and burnt down. The men were killed and the women and children were sold into slavery. The inhabitants of Corinth were mingled comprising of Greeks, Orientals, and Jews. Corinth became a Roman colony. Corinth was surrounded by wall and when it was shaken by an earthquake, and Nero, Vespasian and Harian helped to rebuild that city.

From the port of Lechaion to the North, a road led directly to the central area of Corinth and to the agora. Beyond the basilica to the West on a separate place was the Temple of Apollos, which was built in the sixth century BCE. At the head of the Lechaion Road, splendid propylaea gave access to the agora. At Corinth, drinking vessels (pottery) with inscriptions of names such as Dionysus and Zeus were uncovered. Farther to the North adjacent to the city wall was inscription of Asclepius, the god of healing. On the side of Acrocorinth was a temple of Aphrodite, which, according to Strabo brought allot of wealth to Corinth. There was also an inscription found in the vicinity of the theater at Corinth. On one of the blocks was written the name of Erastus. In Romans 16: 23, which according to J. Finegan, was doubtlessly written in Corinth, Paul mentioned Erastus whom he regarded as the city treasurer. Scholars have maintained that the Erastus of the paving inscription and the one in Romans 16:23 cannot be the same.

Another inscription was found in the vicinity of the Lechaion Road near the agora that mentions a shop or market with the same word in Latin *macellu*, which Paul used in Greek *makellon*, translated "meat market" in I Corinthian 10:25. Another inscription was found on the block of white marble on the Lechanon Road near propylaea. On it was written "Synagogue of the Hebrews." Since the lettering of the word indicates a later date than the time of Paul, it is likely that that synagogue was built after the one that was mentioned in Acts 18:4 where the apostles preached.

Apollos of Alexandria

In my previous discussion, the important role that Alexandrian Christians played in the spread of the Gospel has been discussed. I have stated that Alexandria was one of the most important African intellectual and religious cities. An Alexandrian man named Apollos came to Ephesus as a missionary. There is no doubt that Apollos was an African. It is important to remember that the great and eloquent teacher Apollos in Acts of Apostles 18 and also in Paul's First Epistle to the Corinthians came from Alexandria. It is also significant to mention that the famous Codez Bezae, and uncial, and Bilingual manuscripts of the New Testament (now in Cambridge) mentioned that Apollos received his instruction "in way of the Lord" from Alexandria, his fatherland.[19] Coming from Alexandria, the African Jew was an eloquent man, well trained in rhetoric and philosophy. His method may reflect a gnostic and allegorical method of teaching.[20] Most importantly, he was versed in Scriptures. According to the author of Acts, he had been instructed in the way of the Lord and taught accurately well things concerning Jesus. This means that he was well informed concerning the story of Jesus and His teaching. However, Luke reports that he knew only the baptism of John. This was also the state of the disciples who met at Ephesus in 19:1-7. Aquilla and Priscilla took Apollos home and taught him about the baptism in the name of Jesus.

The fact is that in the pages of the New Testament, the name, Apollos, was not very prominent. That is, his name was not repeated as much as his influence in the New Testament.[21] Instead, what we find in the pages of the New Testament is the description of the eloquent man from Alexandria who was fervent in spirit, and mighty in the scriptures, who came to Ephesus and Corinth. After he was instructed by Aquila and Priscilla in Ephesus, he moved to Corinth where he got involved in strengthening the "infant church by powerfully confuting the Jews" and "showing by the Scriptures that Jesus was the Christ." His presence in Corinth was probably the reason why there was a growth of different parties, which made St. Paul write to the Corinthians to correct the error in I Corinthians 1-4. Apollos was also mentioned in two other places (I Cor. 16:12; and Titus 3:13). The study of Alexandrian antecedent of Apollos, especially his association with Philo of Alexandria and the study of some ideas in the New Testament that appears Philonic will probably support the fact that Apollos was more influential in the New Testament than the number of times his name appeared.[22] Despite his brief stay in Corinth, as an eloquent and mighty teacher who was vast in Scriptures, he was able to impart the knowledge of Scriptures in the mode of African thought to the Pauline churches so much so that after when he had left Corinth, they had the desire that he return to them again (I Cor. 16:12). What I am trying to say is that the influence which Apollos was able to impart on the Pauline churches, is characteristic of Philonic primitive Christian thought. The reason is that Philo of Alexandria was the Jewish writer of the period of Apollos who has left a considerable body of writings, probably more than anyone. At least, we know that before Philo was at the height of his power and fame Apollos was growing up in Alexandria.[23] Finding some of the influences of Apollos may, therefore, involve finding traces of Philonic thought since no disciple of originality would reproduce his teacher verbatim. It will, therefore, be enough to find traces of probable similar ideas and methods, which may not exactly be identical to Philo, in the Gospel and Pauline churches which can be accountable to the presence of Apollos more than any other person's known influence.[24]

We must remember that like Philo, Apollos was mighty in Scriptures as mentioned in Acts 18:24-28. "And a certain Jew named Apollos, born at Alexandria, an eloquent man, and mighty in the scriptures, came to Ephesus" (18:24). It is also clear from what St. Paul said about wisdom, that the Corinthians regarded Apollos' teaching as much more than intellectual than St. Paul's in I Corinthian 1-4. Although he did not find any church because he was not a missionary, his major role was teaching and exposition of the Scriptures. With the high degree of regard given to his teaching and exposition, it is very likely that he brought new ideas and method of interpretations into the churches from Africa.

Now let us start tracing the influences of the African teacher- Apollos. As said earlier, in doing this I will have to begin with the traces of Philonic thought in the New Testament that could be attributed to Apollos. These ideas and thought include the concept of Logos doctrine, the way of accounting for the birth of remarkable persons as both divine and human, allegorical method of interpreting the Old Testament, and eschatological conceptions.

The method of the narrative account of the miraculous birth of John the Baptist and Jesus Christ may be an example of the influence of Apollo's' teaching and exposition. Philo taught the idea that children born according to divine promise or children granted to parents by God as a result of many prayers were children of "divine seed" even though they have human fathers. He saw them as children begotten of God and not by mortals even though they have human fathers. The Gospel of Luke gives the accounts of the birth of John the Baptist and Jesus Christ and presents these as both divine and human. Luke was probably close to Apollo's and knew his teaching as he described it with great interest in the book of Acts. The Gospel of Luke is the earliest book to contain the miraculous birth of John the Baptist and Jesus. Why was Luke so much interested in the account of John the Baptist? He was a companion of Paul and intimate with Apollos, the African teacher and expositor, who was a disciple of John the Baptist. The Gospel of Matthew records the account of the birth of Jesus only. The Gospel of Mark which was written about ten years earlier does not mention these birth accounts of John and Jesus. The possibility then is that these Gospel writers had knowledge of some of the spirit-led teaching of Apollos as he expanded the scripture. No wonder he was said to be fervent in spirit (Acts. 18:24). Apollos' teaching and exposition might be one of the sources of these Gospels.

By the time the Gospel of John was written, the Logos idea had spread through Paul's teaching in the Epistle to the Colosians. Perhaps, this idea had penetrated Pauline churches through Apollos' exposition. It is remarkable that the Gospel of John sees Jesus as the incarnate Logos and at the same time the son of Joseph (Jn. 1:45, 6:42). Here again we see the Philonic concept in which the divine is mingled with the human parentage. Probably by the second century, Apollos' teaching had penetrated Asia Minor and had been adopted by Paul, Luke, Matthew, and John because it was a good truthful African exposition of the Scripture revealed by the spirit of God to his people. Jesus is not less human and is not less divine. This view of Apollos was accepted because it is scriptural; it is supernatural and also contradicts the docetic heresy that reduced the earthly life of Christ to unreality.

In the course of time, this human and divine aspect of Jesus taught by Apollos, the Epistles, and the Gospels developed into the Apostles' Creed and now transmitted to us with apostolic authority that Jesus was the very man and the very God born by the Virgin Mary. Thus, up till today the teaching and the exposition of an African man called Apollos is transmitted to our generation.[25]

Since I have discussed in the previous chapter that there were many African natives in Alexandria living along with Greeks, Romans, and Jews, my readers should not have problem with Apollos being an African. As I have also discussed in the previous chapter the fact that many native Africans took up Jewish citizenship, so also many took up Greek and Roman citizenship. These people also bore either Jewish, Greek, and Roman names. The fact that he was referred to as a Jew should not bring any doubt as to whether he was an African or not. After all when the missionaries came to Africa, those of us who became Christians changed our names to biblical and Jewish names, just as many Africans did in the days of the New Testament. Unfortunately, many Eurocentric scholars have capitalized on the fact that he was called a Jew to deny the Apollos' Africanness. This is not unusual since no nation's achievement has been attributed to other nations like that of Africa.

Despite his eloquence and his being instructed in the way of the Lord, he knew only the baptism of John. This does not mean that he was not a Christian. It means that though he had accepted the baptism of John with water as a symbol of cleansing and repentance, he was not yet aware that Christian converts were baptized in the name of Jesus Christ and the experience of being possessed by the Holy Spirit, which is normally as a consequence of Christian baptismal confession.[26]

Was Apollos a Christian then? The fact that he was fervent in spirit and taught accurately well is evidence that he was a Christian but he was not aware of the tradition of baptism in the name of Christ. It is not that he had not confessed Christ. He has been instructed in the way of the Lord in his home country in Africa. As discussed earlier in the previous chapter, Apollos' home country is one of the centers of the learning in antiquity. He must have attended these schools. Like the African Christians of today, this man was fervent in spirit. He possessed the great zeal and was "boiling" with the energy of the Holy Spirit.

He, therefore, had the desire to pass what he was taught at home to others. This is the normal characteristic of African people. They are action-oriented[27] people and willing to pass along very enthusiastically, what they have received. That accounts for the geometrical growth of Christianity in Africa more than any other continent.

As eloquent and zealous as Apollos was, he was still lacking. However, Aquila and Priscilla explained to him the baptism in the name of Jesus, which he honorably accepted, and continued his teaching. The title of a book, *Every pastor needs a Pastor*[28] is very appropriate here. No one has all the knowledge. No one has absolute knowledge. We learn from one another. One needs to respect the humility of a man who was already instructed in the way of the Lord in one of the famous Alexandrian schools. A man well versed in the scriptures and fervent in spirit still humbles himself enough to receive more instruction

From Aquila and Priscilla. Many of us would not put up with that. We would think we know all. No matter what we know we are still lacking in something.

Apollos continued his missionary journey to Achaia and later to Corinth 19:1-10. In Achaia, he used his knowledge to preach Christ to the Jews and to help them receive Christ through grace.

Endnotes

1. *Diodorus* XV.iii.7. See also *IDB*. IX.786.
2. Ibid. XVI.viii.6.
3. IDB vol. IX. 787.
4. Ibid.
5. Hans Conzelmann, *Acts of the Apostles* (Minneapolis: Fortress Press, 1987), 132.
6. F. P Udoisang, "Africa and Africans in the New Testament," 80.
7. Ibid., See also *The New Bible Dictionary* (Leicester: Intervarsity Fellowship Press, 1962.
8. Ibid. *Antiquity* I.6.4.
9. Gordon J. Wenham, *Word Biblical Commentary*, Gen. 1-5 (Waco: Word Books Publishers, 1967), 230.
10. *Interpreter's Bible*, Vol. IX. , 218-219.
11. Strabo, XIV.632.640.
12. Ibid. 640.
13. Herodotus I.26.
14. Stabo, XIV. 640.
15. Ibid., 641.
16. IDB. E-J, 114-118.
17. Ibid.
18. Ibid.
19. Plumley, "Early Christianity in Egypt," *Palestine Exploration Quarterly* (henceforth PEQ) 89 (1957), 70-81.
20. Vol. IX, 246-247.
21. George A. Barton, "Some Influences of Apollos in the New Testament, I" *Journal of Biblical Literature* 43 (1924), 207-223.
22. Ibid.
23. Ibid. 208. Philo visited Rome before his death in 40. He must have journey to Rome in the year 39-40.
24. Ibid.
25. Ibid. 222
26. IB. Vol. 1X, 1954.
27. I discussed elaborately, the characteristic of religious heritage in among the African people all over the world in my book, *Black American Heritage?* (Waco, Texian Press, 1986). Reprinted by WIPF & Stock Publishers, Eugene, OR. 2001.
28. Louis McBurney, *Every Pastor Needs a Pastor* (Waco, TX: Word Books, 1977)

CHAPTER X

AFRICA AND AFRICANS IN THE EPISTLES TO THE ROMANS

Rufus, The African Pastor in the Church of Rome (Rom. 16:13)

The book of Romans is the longest book of the New Testament letters. It has been the most studied of the Apostle's writings. It has played a major role in the history of the development of Theology in the Christian Church. This letter has influenced many major theologians like Augustine, Abelard, Luther, Calvin, and Barth. This is probably the last book written by Paul with a great development of his theology of grace and justification by faith. This book is more developed theologically as far as the theme of grace and Justification by faith is concerned. It appears that the theological debate in the book of Romans split the Western and the Eastern Church.[1]

As said earlier, of all the Epistles, this is the only book where reference to Africans was made. In Romans 16:13, Paul, toward the conclusion of his letters, sent greetings to some important people in the church in Rome. The idea that chapter 16 is not part of the book of Romans does not make sense. A close examination of 16:21-23 shows that it is typically Pauline. The list of many people whom Paul greets should not be a problem simply because he does not usually greet many named people in his other letters to the churches where he had spent a long time.

The fact is that Paul needed friends to recommend him to others in Rome where he probably has never been.[2] He now includes in his letter of recommendation for Phoebe greetings to various persons in the Roman church, mentioning about twenty-four persons by name. Some of these names are names of people he knew very well and had worked with. Others are names that had come to his attention.³ This may be especially true of the twelve others he speaks of in verses 14-15. Among these names that he seemed to know very well are Priscila, Aquila, Epaenetus, Andronicus, Juia, Ampliatus, Stahys, Apelles, Urbanus, Persis, and Rufus and his mother. It is also remarkable that of those singled out as active in the service of the Lord, seven are women: Prisca, Mary, Junia, Tryphaena, Tryphosa, Persis and Rufus' mother. Paul commended these women for their hard work and activities somewhere else (I Cor. 16:16 and I Thes. 5:12). These women deserve some respect. This shows that women were also active in the church during the early century. Five of these are men: Aquila, Andronicus, Urbanus, Apelles, and Rufus. Among these names some are Greek names such as Andronicus, Apelles, Aristobulus, Asyncritus, Epaenetus, Erastus, Hermes, Jason, Narcisus, Nereus, Olympas, Patrobas, Persis, Philologus, Phlegon, Sosipater, Stachys, Timotheos, Tryphaenam Tryphosa.⁴ Others have Latin names such as Amliatus, Aquila Caius, Julia, Junia, Lucius, Quartus, Rufus, Tertius, Urbanus.⁵ Dunn thinks that there are no Roman names but the Jews names probably includes Aquila and Prisca, Mary, Rufus and his mother.⁶ But only two names are mentioned that are Hebrew names, such as Mary and Herodion.⁷ These persons greeted in this letter of recommendation and commendation serves as list of people on whom Phoebe could call upon in Rome for hospitality and assistance.

One should not disassociate this chapter sixteen from the rest of the book because Paul "rarely greets individuals as he does" when he wrote to other churches. The reason may be that he does not want to single out some individual and neglect others in the churches he established himself. However, the situation is undoubtedly different here since Paul did not establish the Roman church where he sent this letter. However, he knew some of the key people and had worked with them.

A great deal of research has been done on the geographical distribution of these names with the hope of establishing whether these names are familiar names in Rome during the first century. The result of these researches is that many of these names are familiar names and are found throughout the empire. Very unfortunately indeed, is the fact that the majority of the Eurocentric biblical scholars sees class and social status in this chapter and tries to analyze the names that belong to slaves and freemen.⁸ Rufus was also among the names said to belong to the slaves. Certainly that was not the intention of Paul. Paul was not interested in who is of lower class and who is of higher class. To him all Christians are one in Christ. Interestingly what Paul was trying to do is to "single out for commendation those who bore a firmly established name for conspicuously Christian character."⁹ Among these important people was one Rufus who was regarded as "chosen in the Lord." It is noteworthy that among the people Paul sent salutation, none was described as "chosen in the Lord" but Rufus (13). The question that can be legitimately asked at this time is, who is that Rufus? Rufus is a Latin name found very often in the Roman society. D.G.

Dunn strongly believes that this Rufus is related to and the son of Simon who carried the cross of Christ to Golgotha.[10]

Lightfoot also accepts the opinion that this Rufus is the same as the Rufus of Mark 15:21. According to him the fact that Mark alone of the four Gospel is the one that mentioned Simon as the father of Rufus and Alexander shows that someone called Rufus has held a very prominent position among the Christians at Rome. Despite scholar's opinion that Rufus is a common name in Rome, it is fair to identify this Rufus of St. Paul with the Rufus of Mark. To him this stands as a balanced scholarly judgment.[11]

In order to answer this question, we need to make reference to the Gospel. In Mark 15:21 we learned of a man called Simon of Cyrene, which I have already discussed in detail. While Matthew is silent about Simon's family, Mark made mention of some of them as Alexander and Rufus. These two were said to be Simon's children. I have mentioned the activities of this Simon of Cyrene who was forced to carry the cross for Jesus. I have mentioned of the fact that after his experience in carrying the cross of Christ, waiting and watching Jesus on the cross, listening to his words on the cross and seeing him dying, he believed. He probably interacted with the disciples and later became a missionary to other Gentiles' cities. He participated in establishing the Church in Antioch. Simon and his son were teachers and prophets in the church in Antioch. Simon was also one of the teachers and prophets who laid hands and ordained Paul before embarking on his missionary journey to the Gentiles (Acts 13:1).

This man who is a teacher and prophet, with such a strong faith, must have taught his sons in the way of the Lord. They probably became missionaries to other Gentiles Churches. While Simon, his father was in Antioch as a teacher and prophet, his son Rufus was in Rome as a minister of the church. Note how Paul addressed Rufus: "chosen in the Lord." Admittedly, the Greek word *eklektos* can apply to all Christians as the word *agapetos* was used by Paul in Romans 16:5.[12] This indicates that Rufus was well known as a person specially chosen for a specific and significant task such as his father did by carrying the cross. This is because the word *eklektos* is also used of individual chosen for some special task as is in Psalm 18:26, II John1 and Wisdom of Solomon 3:14. So the idea put forward by many Eurocentric scholars that the phrase "chosen in the Lord" does not mean anything special is an attempt to strip Rufus of the special status attributive to him by Paul who knew him well. This may also be an attempt to deAfricanize the New Testament. On the basis of the fact that Rufus was mentioned in Romans 16:13 it appears be the son of Simon who carried the cross of Jesus. He then must have been from Cyrene in Africa. Their family was well known to Paul if one remembers that his father laid hand on him before his missionary journey. Later, legends have it that the same Rufus became the Bishop of Thebes.[13] In the light of the above, Fitmyer's idea that this Rufus is not the same Rufus mentioned in Mark 15:21 and that the name Rufus is a common Latin name for slaves is therefore untenable. Paul's special mention of Rufus as "chosen in the Lord," or "the elect one," shows that Paul wanted to single him out because of his outstanding Christian character. Paul also greeted Rufus' mother and called her his mother.[14] It shows again that the family was well known and that the woman probably had shown some hospitality to Paul sometimes. Paul recalled many occasions of comforting hospitality from Rufus' mother during his previous travels. Like any other African, Rufus' mother demonstrated that characteristic of love and hospitality to Paul on his missionary journey as they did to the colonial masters who eventually enslaved Africans. In many occasions she probably did what Lydia, the African woman did for Paul.

Endnotes

[1] Raymond Brown, *an Introduction to the New Testament*, 259. See also J.D Godsey, and R. Jewett, *Interpretation*, 34 (1980), 3-16, 17-31.
[2] Raymond Brown, *An Introduction to the New Testament*, 375.
[3] Joseph Fitzmyer, *Romans: Anchor Bible*, 1993), 734
[4] Ibid.
[5] Ibid.
[6] J. D.G Dunn, *Romans: Word Biblical Commentary* (Dallas: Word Books Publ., 1988), 900.
[7] Fitzmyer, *Romans: Anchor Bible*, 734
[1] See J.D.Gunn, *Romans*, 900.
[8] *The Interpreter's Bible*, Vol. IX, 1954, 661.
[9] D.G Gun, *Romans*, 900
[10] Cranfied, *The Epistle to the Romans, International Critical Commentary* Vol.2 (Edinburgh: T & T Clark, 1979), 793-94
[11] James DG. Dunn, *Word Biblical Commentary, Romans 9-16*, Vol. 38 (Dallas: Word Books Pub. 1988), 897.
[12] Fitzmyer, *Romans*, 741.
[13] Douglas J. Moo, *The Epistle to the Romans* (Michigan: WMB Eerdmans Pub. 1996), 925.

CHAPTER XI

CONCLUSION

In the preceding work, I have examined Africa and Africans in the New Testament Bible. From this examination, I have pointed out that in the New Testament Africa and Africans are mentioned more frequently than any other nation except Israel. They mentioned them in every genre of the New Testament literature. They mentioned them in the book classified as the Gospel, the historical books of the Acts of the Apostles, and the Epistles.

It is gratifying to know that while some of the Jews were trying to kill the infant Jesus, the first people to announce the virgin birth and the Kingship of Jesus prophetically, were Africans (Matt 2:1-12). Africa became a place of refuge for the savior, as it has been for ages in biblical history. God did not make a mistake in choosing Africa of all the nations available. Of all the people present watching Jesus going through the excruciating pain of carrying the heavy cross after being beaten, only the black man from Cyrene, Africa, showed a sympathetic face and was forced to help Jesus carry that cross on Jesus behalf and on behalf of the entire world (Mark 15:21; Matt. 27:32; Lk. 23:36). In fact, the evangelists Mark and Matthew, the writers of the Gospel of Mark and Matthew, who probably preached and died in Africa, according to ancient tradition, may probably, be Africans. Further research may authenticate this.

In the historical books, which narrated the history of the early Christian church, we have the highest number of reference to Africa and Africans in the New Testament. Right from the time of the Pentecost when the Holy Ghost came upon the people, Africans who were present there and became one of the recipients of the Holy Ghost (Acts 2:5-13, 37-41) have been aggressively involved in the spreading of the Gospel by teaching, preaching, and laying of hands throughout the known world. This has been evident where African teachers and prophets spread the Gospel to Antioch (Acts 13:1); Stephen who was likely to be an African preached in the synagogue full of Africans before the jealous people stirred up others to murder him (Acts 6-7); Before the Gospel was committed to written form, the Old Testament which was the main Scripture of that period was already in the hands of an African Official Treasurer of one of African Kingdoms, called "Ethiopian eunuch" (Acts 8:26-40).[1] He was an educated man and was in possession of the book of Isaiah. The truth is that Scripture has been having great impact upon the life of Africans even before the Europeans ever heard of the Gospel (the so called Ethiopian Eunuch in Acts 8). It is also remarkable that Lydia, usually viewed as a European woman convert may likely be an Africans. She, like the black people all over the world, she expressed her generosity to preachers in order to further preach the Gospel of Jesus Christ.

Rufus, who was the son of the African man, Simon of Cyrene, may have been one of the preachers in the church in Rome (Rom. 16:13). Paul the Apostle, the greatest of the Bible writers was in an occasion accused of being like an African revolutionist in his zeal (Acts 21:38). Could Paul be an African? Further research will tell some day.

The truth is that the background of African Christianity is the Bible. They were present in the biblical events to express their zeal and culture. Perhaps, that is the reason why Christianity is growing at a geometrical rate in Africa to the extent that someone called the continent of Africa the "laboratory of the world" as far as Christianity is concerned.

From the examination of the New Testament above, it is certain that the Bible holds no prejudice against any race or color. The readers and the interpreters are the people propagating the prejudice against Africans all over the world. God is against racism and abhors prejudice. Africa and Africans have participated fully in the drama of redemption and they are not latecomers in the preaching of the Gospel. They have contributed socially, economically, and religiously to the life of the people in the biblical period.

It is my hope that the questions that were asked in the introduction of this book have been answered. Let me repeat these questions. Is it correct to say that Western missionaries and explorers brought Christianity to Africa? Is Christianity a White man's religion as some people claim? Why did the biblical writers take time always to give specific identification to the people of African descent as people from Africa whenever they are mentioned in the pages of the New Testament? Why is the church growing geometrically, that is, at the rate of 16,400 Christians per day in Africa? [2] Why did Dr. Kwame Bediako, regards Africa as the "laboratory of the world" as far as Christianity is concerned?[3] I have tried to present evidence that requires a closer look at the pages of the book of the Old and New Testament and what they say about Africa and Africans show that it is not correct that the Western missionaries and explorers brought Christianity to Africa. This book has also demonstrated that Christianity is not a

White man's religion, but it is also an African religion. When Christianity was born, Africa and Africans were not excluded. The line of genealogy of Jesus includes Africans. Many Africans participated in the early spread of Christianity to all over the ancient world. Up till today, Africans are involved in the spread of Christianity in every continent of the world, especially in Europe and North America. Wherever Africans are found they carry their culture and their vibrant version of Christianity along with them. No wonder Benjamin Zephaniah, a Caribbean poet says, "You can take me out of Africa, but you can't take Africa out of me."[4] "There is an increasing impact of African influence on Christianity not only on the religious mapping of Africa but also on religious movements globally."[5] Jehu-Appiah is correct when he insists that,

> Christianity was not brought to Africa by Western explorers and missionaries some of whom 'robbed the Africans of their personhood once they became Christians'. On the contrary, Christianity predates the Western missions. From the time of Pentecost, trade and traffic between Palestine, Rome and Africa, Simon of Cyrene forced to carry Jesus' cross, the Ethiopian Eunuch being baptized, Christian churches and martyrs in North Africa, the establishment of Christianity in Egypt and Ethiopia around 600-all confirming that the biblical stories were told and the 'universal attributes of God' were taught in Africa long before the arrival of white missionaries.[6]

Finally, I believe that the biblical writers did not make any mistake of personally identifying Africans who were involved in every aspect of Judaism and Christianity; they did that because they recognized their zeal and enthusiasm. There was no prejudice against any black race in the New Testament because the biblical writers did not believe that God made any mistake by creating them black. There was no question of inferiority then. This can be attested to by the biblical writers mentioning Africa and Africans more than any other nation (42 times) in the New Testament. This shows the importance of Africa and Africans in the Bible.

Endnotes

1. My readers should remember that the word Ethiopia does not necessarily mean the modern Ethiopian country, though it may include her.
2. Ronald A. Nathan, "Pan-Africanism: What of the Twenty-First Century? A British Perspective," *Black Theology in Britain,* Issue 4, 2000, 19.
3. Kwame Bediako, (Christianity in Africa), 252.
4. Benjamin Zephaniah, BBC Radio 2, 1995.
5. Roswith Gerloff, "An African Continuum in Variation: The African Christian Diaspora in Britain," in *Black Theology in Britain*, Issue 4, 2000, 106-107.
6. Ibid. 107.

BIBLIOGRAPHY

Adamo, David Tuesday. *Africa and Africans in the Old Testament.* San Franco: Christian University Press, 1998. Reprinted by WIPF and Stock Publishers, Eugene, Oregon, 2001.

--------- *Black American Heritage.* Waco, Texian Press, 1985. Reprinted by WIPF and Stock Publishers, Eugene, Oregon, 2001

Beaskey, J, etal. *An Introduction to the Bible.* Nashville: Abingdon Press, 1991.

Benton, William ed. *The New Encyclopedia Britanica* Vol.1 15th edition. William Benton, 1973.

Bernal, Martin. Black Athena: *The Fabrication of Ancient Greece, 1785-1985.*vol. 1. London : Free Association Books, 1987.

Boykin Sanders, "In Search of a Face for Simon the Cyrene," *The Recovery of Black Presence: An Interdisciplinary Exploration,* Randall Bailey and Jacquelyn Grant (editors) Nashville, Abingdon Press, 1995.

Bright, John. *A History of Israel.* Philadelphia: Westminster Press, 1972.

Brown, Raymond. *An Introduction to the New Testament.* New York: Doubleday, 1997.

Metzger, M B. *The Canon of the New Testament Its Origin, Development, and Significance.* Oxford: Clarendon Press, 1997

Budge, E.A Wallis. *The Egyptian Sudan.* vol. 1. New York: AMS Press, 1976.

Budge, Wallis. *The Queen of Sheba and Her Son Menyelek.* London: London University Press, 1932.

Conzelmann, Hans. *Acts of the Apostles. Fortress Press,* 1987.

Copher, Charles. *Black Biblical Studies.* Chicago: Black Light Fellowship, 1993.

Cranfield, *The Epistle to the Romans: International Critical Commentary* Vol. 2. Edinburgh: T &T Clark, 1979.

Davis, Paul. E. "Jesus and the Role of the Prophet," *Journal of Biblical Literature* 64 (1948), 240-254.

Diop, Cheikh Anta. *African Origin of Egyptian Civilization: Myth or Reality?* Trans. By Mercer Cook, Westport: Lawrence Hill & Co., 1974.

Douglas, J.D. (Chief editor) *The Illustrated Bible Dictionary.* Part 1` Leicester, UK : Intervasity Press, 1980.

Dunn J.D.G. Romans: *Word Biblical Commentary.* Dallas: Word Books Publisher, 1988.

Dunston, Alfred G. *The Black Man in the Old Testament and Its World.* Philadelphia: Dorrance & Co., 1974

Etheridge, J.W. *The Targums of Onkelos and Jonathan Ben Uzziel on the Pentateuch I-II.* New York: Ktav Press, 1964.

Felder, Cain Hope. Cultural Ideology, Afrocentrism and Biblical Interpretation," *Black Theology: A Documentary History.* Edited by James Cone and G.S Wilmore, Vol. 2. New York: Orbis, 1993.

_____ (editor) *Stony the Road We Trod.* Minneapolis: Fortress Press, 1991.

-----------------Troubling Biblical Waters: Race, Class, and Family Maryknoll, New York: Orbis Book, 1989.

_____General Editor, *The Original African Heritage Study Bible* Nashville, Ten: Winston –Derek Publishers, Inc., 1998.

Fohrer, Sellin. *Introduction to the Old Testament.* Nashville: Abingdon Press, 1965.

Galpaz Pnina. "The Reign of Jeroboam and the Extent of Egyptian Influence," *Biblische Notizen* 60 (1991), 13-19.

Gray, John. *I & II Kings.* Philadelphia: Westminster Press, 1963.

Gunther, John. J. "The Association of Mark and Barnabas with Egyptian Christianity," *The Evangelical Quarterly,* 54 (1982):219-233.

Guy, H.A. New Testament Prophecy Its Origin and Significance. London: Epiworth Press, 1947.

Hansberry, Leo. *Africa and Africans as Seen by Classical Writers.* Washington DC: Howard University Press, 1977.

Harvey, A.E. *The New English Bible: Companion to the Gospel.* Oxford: Oxford University Press, 1972

Selected Bibliography

Harris, Joseph E. *Africa and Africans as Seen by the Classical Writers.* Washington DC: Howard University Press, 1901.

Harrison, J.K. *Introduction to the Old Testament.* Grand Rapids: William B. Eerdmans Publishing Co., 1979.

Henchmen, Ernst. *Acts of the Apostles A Commentary.* Philadelphia: Westminster Press, 1965.

Holy Bible, The African American Jubilee Edition With Supplementary Materials. New York: American Bible Society, 1999.

Hubbard, D.A. "Queen of Sheba," *New Bible Dictionary.* Ed. J. Douglas, Wheaton: Tyndale House, 1982.

Hyman, Mark. *Blacks who died for Jesus.* Nashville: Winston-Derek Publishers, Inc. 1983.

"Men and Women of Color," *Holy Bible, Heritage Edition.* Langley Park, Maryland: International Bible Inc., 1977.

Jackson, John. *Ethiopia and the Origin of Civilization.* Baltimore: Black Classic Press, 1939.

Jervel, Jacob. *New Testament Theology: The Theology of Acts of the Apostles.* Cambridge: Cambridge University Press, 1996.

Johnson, Luke Timothy. The Acts of the Apostles (Collegeville, Minnesota: Michael Glazier Liturgical Press, 1992.

Johnstone, R.L. *Religion and Society in Interaction.* Englewood Cliffs: Prentice Hall, Inc. 1975.

Keener, C and Usry, Glenn. *Black Man's Religion.* Downers Grove: Illinois, 1996.

Keener, Craig. *Matthew: The IVP New Testament Commentary Series.* Dowers Grove: Intervasity Press, 1997.

Luz, Ulrich,. *New Testament Theology: The Theology of the Gospel of Matthew.* Cambridge: Cambridge University Press, 1993.

McKim, Donald K. (Ed) Historical Handbook of Major Biblical Interpreters. Downers Grove: InterVersity Press, 1998

Mellink, M.J. "Cyrene," Interpreters' *Dictionary of the Bible* edited by George Buttrick. Nashville: Abingdon Press, 1986.

Moo, Douglas J. *The Epistle to the Romans.* Michigan: William Eerdmans Publisher, 1996.

Ndubukwu, C.O G "Some Concepts of the African Literature," Unpublished PhD Thesis, University of Ibadan, Nigeria. 1979.

O'Toole, R.F. "Philip and the Ethiopian Eunuch (Acts VIII 25-40)," *Journal of New Testament Studies* 17 (1983). 25-34.

Paterson, John. "The Old Testament World," *The Bible History*, ed William Barclay. Nashville: Abingdon Press, 1968.

Pfeiffer, Robert H. *History of the New Testament Times*. London: Adam and Charles Black, nd.

Perry W.J. *The Growth of Civilization*, 2nd edition. Harmonsworth: Penguin Books, 1939.

Perkins, Theme. *The New Interpreters' Bible*. Vol VIII. Nashville: Abingdon Press, 1995.

Petrie, Flinders. *The Making of Egypt*. London: Sheldon Press, 1939.

Plumley, J.M. "Early Christianity in Egypt," *Palestine Exploration Quarterly*, 89 (1957) 70-81

Pritchard, James. *Ancient Near Eastern Text Relating to the Old Testament*, 3rd Edition. Princeton: Princeton University Press, 1969.

Pritchard, James. *Solomon and Sheba*. London: Phaidon Press, 1974.

Rashidi, Ronoko, "African Presence in Early Asian Civilizations: A Historical Overview," *African Presence in Early Asia*. Ivan Van Sertima ed. New Brunswick: Transaction Books, 1985.

Rawlinson, Henry. *History of Herodotus*, Book I trans. George Rawlinson. New York: Tudor Publishing, 1956.

Robinson, J. *Archaeology and Religion of Israel*. 5th Edition. Doubleday Anchor Book, 1959.

Robinson, J. *First Book of Kings*. Cambridge: Cambridge University Press, 1972.

Smith, Abraham. "Do you Understand What You are Reading?" A Literary Critical Reading of the Ethiopian (Kushite) Episode (Acts 8:26-40). *Journal of Interdenominational Cente*, 22 (1994): 48-70.

Snape, H.C. "The Fourth Gospel, Ephesus, and Alexandria," *Harvard Theological Review* XLVII (Jan. 1954), 1 3.

Snowden, Frank. *Blacks in Antiquity: Ethiopians in the Greco Roman Experience*. Cambridge: Cambridge University Press, 1970.

Soares-Prabhu, George M. "Jesus in Egypt," *Estudios Biblicos* 50 (1992) 225-249.

Stieglitz, R.R. "Long Distance Seafaring in Ancient Near East," *Biblical Archaeologist*. Vol 47, No 3 (1984), 1334-1342.

Thayer, Joseph H. " Niger," *The New Thayers Greek-English Lexicon of the New Testament*. Laffayette: The Book Factory, 1979.

Tilley, M A. *The Bible in Christian North Africa: The Donatist World*. Minneapolis: Augsburg Fortress, 1997

Udoisang, Friday. "Africa and Africans in the New Testament," Unpublished M.A Thesis, Delta State University, Abraka, Nigeria, 1998.

Ullendorf, Edward. *Ethiopian and the Bible: The Schweich Lectures of the British Academy*. Oxford: Oxford University Press, 1968.

_____ "Candace (Acts VIII.27) and he Queen of Sheba," *Journal of the New Testament Studies* 2 (1956), 53-56.

Wenham Gordon J. *Word Biblical Commentary, Genesis 1-5*. Waco: Word Books Publishers, 1967.

Index

Abraham, 43, 45, 54, 58, 84, 85, 93
Achaia, 102,108
Act of the Apostles, 62, 78, 79, 86, 93, 108, 111
Acts of Scillitan martyrs, 18
Africa and Africans, 3, 5, 6, 7, 52, 56, 58, 60, 68, 82, 111, 112, 113, 114
Africa and theicans in the Old Testament, 3, 5, 6, 7
Africa, 1, 2, 3, 5, 7, 8, 9, 10, 11 13, 14, 15, 16, 17, 18, 21, 45, 52, 53, 54, 55, 56, 58, 59, 60, 62, 64, 65, 66, 67, 68, 72, 75, 79, 81, 82, 83, 84, 85, 87, 89, 90, 93, 98, 105, 107, 108, 110, 111, 112, 113, 114
African and Africans, 108
African Christianity, 112
African martyr, 83
African Minister of Finance, 87, 93
African products, 55, 66,
African Queen, 52, 61, 68,
African wisdom, 83, 85
African wise men, 52, 53,
African woman, 95
Agade, 5
Akhenaton, 85

Alexander the Great, 45, 71, 72, 73, 81, 89, 91, 96, 101, 109
Alexandria, 9, 11, 12, 13, 14, 15, 16, 17, 18, 19, 20, 81, 83, 91, 104, 105, 106,
Ancient Egypt, 45, 46, 47
Antioch, 73, 81, 83, 91, 92, 93, 109, 110, 112
Aphrike, 1
Aphrodite, 103
Apollos of Alexandria, 11, 13, 14, 16, 100, 103, 104, 105, 106, 107, 108
Aquila, 104 107, 108
Aquilla and priscilla, 104
Arabia, 64, 90
Arius, 17
Artemission, 101
Asenath, 59
Ashurbanipal, 44
Asiatic Ethiopians, 6
Assyrians, 4, 6, 44, 45, 60, 66
Athanasius, 17, 19, 20
Augustine of Hippo, 20
Babylon, 6, 45, 57, 58
Bailey, 54, 65, 75
Barnabas, 11, 12, 18, 21, 73, 78, 91, 92

Basilides, 16, 73
Bethlehem, 52, 55, 56
Bishop of Besiers, 53,
Black, 2, 3, 4, 14, 20, 21
Cain Hope Felder, 8
Carpocrates and Valentinus, 16
Carthage, 9
Christology, 60, 66
Church, 78, 92, 102, 107, 108, 109
Cicero, 10
Clement of Alexandria, 11, 12, 15, 17
Coptic, 45, 74
Corinth, 92, 100, 102, 103 104, 108
Cornelius, 78, 88
Council of Ephesus, 102
Cushit, 10
Cyprian of Carthage, 15, 17, 18, 19
Cyrenaica, 74
Cyrene, 6, 18, 19, 52, 69, 70, 72, 73, 75, 80, 81, 83, 91, 109, 110, 111,
Cyril of Alexandria, 20
Decius, 102
Deissmann, 78, 79
Diaspora, 3, 5, 6
Didymus the Blind, 18
Diodorus Sicilus, 11, 54, 68, 83, 90, 96, 108
Dionysus, 54, 103
Eastern Ethiopians, 10, 11
Edonite, 59
Edward Ullendorf, 64, 65, 93
Egypt, 3, 5, 6, 43, 44, 45, 46, 47, 48, 53, 54, 55, 56, 57,58, 59, 60, 64, 67, 68, 74, 75, 83, 84, 85, 90, 93, 98, 114
Egyptian Civilization, 5, 7
Egyptians, 43, 44, 45, 46, 47, 48, 54, 66
Elephantine, 72, 81
Emmanuel, 61
Ephesus, 100, 101, 102, 104, 105

Ethiopia, 1, 2, 5, 6, 7, 8, 9, 10, 11, 12, 13, 14, 19, 47, 53, 54, 55, 62, 63, 64, 65, 79, 82, 87, 88, 90, 93, 98, 114,
Ethiopian Eunuch, 79, 82, 87, 89, 93, 112 114
Ethiopian tradition, 63, 66
Ethiopian, 44, 53, 63, 65, 66, 82, 87, 88, 89, 90, 93, 112,114
Eudoxus of Cyzicus, 11
Euesbius, 2, 16, 17
Euro-americans, 3, 7
Eurocentric, 3, 4, 5, 7, 46, 47, 81, 98, 107, 109, 110
Eusebius, 12
Falashas, 7, 82
Galileans, 80
Gentiles, 53, 55, 61, 73, 77, 78, 80, 91, 92, 109, 110
George Rawlinson, 6, 47
Gerald Masseey, 47
Gifts, 52
Gnosticism, 16
Golgotha, 70, 72, 81, 83, 109
Gospel, 5, 51, 52, 61, 68, 69, 73, 74, 75, 78, 80, 82, 85, 88, 104, 105, 106, 109, 111, 112, 113
Greco- Romans, 8, 12, 71, 89, 90, 91
Greek, 1, 2, 8, 9, 11, 15, 17, 18, 45, 51, 52, 54, 71, 72, 74, 81, 87, 91, 96, 101, 103, 106, 107, 108, 110
Gudea of Lagash, 5
Hamites, 98
Hansberry, 64, 68
Hebrews, 58, 60, 65, 79, 84, 85
Herod, 52, 55, 56, 58, 91
Herodotus, 10, 13, 18
Hesiod, 9, 13
Hexapla, 17
Hittites, 44
Holy Ghost, 80, 81, 83, 112
Horn of Africa, 64

Index

Hyksos, 8, 9, 43, 45, 47
I and II John, 79
Irenaeus, 73, 75
Islamic tradition, 63
Israel, 4, 6, 44, 51, 54, 56, 57, 58, 59, 60, 61, 62, 63, 66, 67, 75, 78, 82, 83, 84, 93, 111
Jacob, 57, 59, 64, 86
James, 6, 78, 92, 112
Jeroboam, 44
Jeroboam, 59, 68
Jerusalem Bible Version, 20
Jerusalem, 11, 12, 13, 14, 15, 19, 20, 45, 52, 57, 60, 65, 72, 77, 80, 81, 82, 83, 87, 88, 90, 91, 92, 93
Jesus, 7, 51, 52, 53, 55, 56, 57, 58, 60, 61, 67, 68, 79, 80, 81, 82, 83, 88, 89, 91, 92, 99, 104, 105, 106, 107, 109, 110, 111, 112, 113, 114
Jewish tradition, 57, 62, 63
Jewish, 57, 61, 62, 63, 66, 72, 77, 81, 82, 85, 87, 91, 92, 96, 98, 99, 105, 107
Jews, 4, 5, 7, 55, 60, 61, 77, 78, 80, 81, 84, 91, 92, 96, 99, 103, 104, 106, 108, 111
Joseph, 43, 44, 55, 56, 58, 106, 112
Judaism, 79, 82, 91, 114
Kebra Nagast, 65, 66
King James Version, 2, 13, 20
King of Ethiopia, 62
Kwame Bediako, 5, 8, 113, 114
Lemba tribe, 82
Libya, 6
Libyans, 81, 93, 98
Lucius, 73, 84, 93, 98, 108
Luke, 7, 12 13, 14, 51, 52, 61, 65, 67, 51, 52, 61, 65, 67, 77, 78, 88, 89, 90, 98, 99, 104, 106
Luke-acts, 77
LXX, 13, 19, 88, 93
Lydia, 95, 96, 98, 99, 100, 110, 112

Macedonia, 95, 96
Macedonians, 98
Magan, 1, 5, 6
Magi, 52, 53, 54, 55, 56, 68
Manetho, 47, 85
Mark, 7, 11, 12, 13, 14, 15, 21, 106, 109, 110, 111, 14 15, 19, 51, 52, 61, 69, 71, 72, 73, 74, 75, 81, 84
Mary, 55, 60, 102, 106, 108
Mathew, 7, 12 13, 14, 15, 20, 51, 52, 56, 57, 58, 60, 61 62 65 67, 68, 70 71, 72, 75, 82, 90, 106, 109, 111
Mathias, 80
Mediterranean, 44, 47, 72, 91, 101
Meluhha, 1, 5, 6
Menelik, 63
Messiah, 55, 56, 57, 60
Middle kingdom, 43, 47
Moses, 59, 79, 83, 84, 85
Mother of Mankind, 1
Nag Hammadi, 73, 75
Nazareth, 56, 57
Nelchior, 53, 68
Nero, 89, 103
New kingdom, 44
New Testament, 1, 2, 3, 4, 5, 6, 7, 15, 14, 16, 17, 18, 19, 20, 51, 52, 65, 68, 69, 77, 78, 79 86, 93, 97, 104, 105, 107, 108, 110, 111, 112, 113, 114
Niger, 2, 13, 14, 19, 20, 72, 73, 80, 92
Nigeria, 75, 84
Nile valley, 5, 7
North Africa, 4, 9, 15, 17, 18, 19, 20, 18, 72, 73, 75, 98, 114
Nubians, 46, 48
Old Testament, 2, 3, 4, 5, 6, 7, 9, 14, 17, 19, 21, 52, 53, 54, 57, 58, 60, 61, 62, 65, 68, 75, 78, 81, 87, 89, 90, 93, 98, 105, 112
Origen, 15, 16, 17, 20

Palestine, 44, 64, 91, 113
Pan-babylonians, 5
Pantaenus, 15, 16, 17
Paul, 73, 78, 79, 80, 88, 91, 92, 95, 96, 98, 99, 100 101, 103, 104, 105, 106, 108, 109, 110, 112,
Pauline letters, 79
Pentaenus, 17
Pentapolis, 18
Pentecost, 80, 81, 82, 112, 113
Persian, 45, 53, 98,100
Peter, 77, 79, 80, 81, 92
Pharaoh, 10
Pharisees, 61, 82
Philip II, 96
Philip, 62, 83, 96
Philippi, 95, 96, 98, 99
Philo, 81, 104, 105
Pilate, 70
Pliny the Elders, 12
Portipharah, 59
Proselytes, 80
Psalm, 110
Psalm, 53, 55, 93
Psammeticus, 45
Punt, 6
Queen of Sheba, 52, 54, 55, 61, 62, 63, 64, 65, 66, 67, 68, 90, 93
Queen of the South, 52, 65
Refuge, 55
Richard Lepsius, 7
River Nile, 9
Romans, 2, 8, 12, 19, 45, 54, 70, 71, 73, 79, 80, 81, 82, 91, 96, 101, 102, 103, 106, 108, 110, 112
Rome, 77, 91, 101, 102, 107, 108, 109, 110, 112, 113

Rufus, 12, 71, 73, 80, 81, 84, 107, 108, 109, 110, 112
Sabach, 11
Semitic culture, 8
Semitic, 43
Shabaka, 44
Shishak, 44
Simon of Cyrene, 69, 71, 72, 73, 52, 109, 112, 113
Simon, 52, 69, 70, 71, 72, 73, 74, 75, 80, 81, 83, 109, 110, 112, 113
Stephen, 82, 83, 84, 86, 91, 112
Strabo, 9, 10, 11, 12, 18, 54, 68, 89, 93, 100, 102, 103, 108
Sudan, 1, 7, 13, 14
Synagogue of Hebrews, 103
Syria, 91, 64
Talmud, 63
The American Standard Version, 13, 20
The Good New Bible, 13, 20
The New International Version, 13
Thebes, 43, 44, 110
Theodosius II, 102
Theogony, 9
Theophilus, 77, 80
Thyatira, 95, 98, 99
Tiglath-Pileser, 64
Troas, 95
Uganda, 56
Upper Egypt, 44, 47, 73, 75
Venerable Bede, 53
Wallis Budge, 7
Western mission, 113
Yahweh, 6, 54, 59, 85, 93
Yoruba, 84
Zeus, 55, 103
Zoroaster, 53

www.ingramcontent.com/pod-product-compliance
Lightning Source LLC
Chambersburg PA
CBHW021129300426
44113CB00006B/355